Spinstered

Surviving Singleness After 40

Sharyn Kopf

LoJo Publishing
2015

Copyright © 2015 by Sharyn Kopf

All rights reserved. This book or any portion thereof may not be reproduced or used in any manner whatsoever without the express written permission of the publisher except for the use of brief quotations in a book review or scholarly journal.

First Printing: 2015

ISBN: 978-1511534208

LoJo Publishing
803 E. Sandusky Ave.
Bellefontaine, OH 43311

www.sharynkopf.wordpress.com
www.girlsnightin40.com

Unless otherwise noted Scripture quotations are taken from the New King James Version. Copyright © 1982 by Thomas Nelson, Inc. Used by permission. All rights reserved.

Scripture quotations marked (ESV) are from the ESV® Bible (The Holy Bible, English Standard Version®), copyright © 2001 by Crossway, a publishing ministry of Good News Publishers. Used by permission. All rights reserved.

Scripture quotations marked (NIV) are taken from the Holy Bible, New International Version®, NIV®. Copyright © 1973, 1978, 1984, 2011 by Biblica, Inc.™ Used by permission of Zondervan. All rights reserved worldwide.

Special discounts are available on quantity purchases by corporations, associations, educators, and others. For details, contact the publisher at the above listed address.

U.S. trade bookstores and wholesalers: Please contact LoJo Publishing, tel: (937) 407-7943 or email sharynkopf@gmail.com.

To all the single women who have been a part of my life—your laughter and tears, hopes and fears touched my heart and encouraged me to keep writing.

This is for you.

4

Contents

Acknowledgements 7

Chapter 1—Introduction 9

Chapter 2—My So-called Single Life: *Sweet Dreams* 17

Chapter 3—Denial: *I'm All Right* 29

Chapter 4—Disbelief: *I Still Haven't Found What I'm Looking For* 49

Chapter 5—Bargaining: *Love the One You're With* 77

Chapter 6—Guilt: *Lonely Is the Night* 99

Chapter 7—Anger: *Love Is a Battlefield* 129

Chapter 8—Depression: *Open Arms* 147

Chapter 9—Hope: *(Everything I Do) I Do It for You* 167

Postscript—To Married Women: *That's What Friends Are For* 191

Endnotes 207

6

Acknowledgements

This book has been a journey. One that has crossed state lines, river valleys, and mountain peaks. As a lifelong single woman, I've had many opportunities in my travels to meet all kinds of people with all kinds of ideas about marriage and singleness. Many of them contributed to the thoughts expressed here.

Of course I have to mention the numerous single friends I've had over the years, especially those in Indiana, Colorado, and Ohio. Their honesty and vulnerability helped me work through many of the stages of grief and gave me stories and insights that have been invaluable to this process.

I also have to thank my family. I never would have made it to this point without their encouragement. From my talented sister, Susie Jarvis, who designed the gorgeous book cover, to my Dad's continued love and support, their fingerprints are all over this book. Then there are my nieces and nephew, who fill my heart with so much joy—their hugs are like cozy blankets of hope.

Many others helped, from my beta readers—Kathy Gerstorff, Elizabeth Markoff, Esther Tyler, and Kay Headley—to my favorite editor, Asheritah Ciuciu.

Most of all I'm grateful to God, who has been forever faithful, even when I stubbornly thought I knew better than He did. I'm so glad I was wrong.

Thank you!

8

Introduction

I am more single today than I have ever been ...
—Catie Delaney, *Spinstered the Novel*

This is a love story.

Though it took me forever to realize it, this truly is a love story, complete with a hero who fights for the girl and refuses to let her go and loves her unconditionally.

It also has plenty of tears and a rollercoaster of emotions. Not the fun kind either. In fact, the whole story teeters on the edge of heartbreak.

In other words, it's not a romance. It doesn't even have a happy ending. More like a happy beginning ... because it's far from over.

Writing this story wasn't easy for me because I wrote it from a place of grief. In the first seven chapters, you will see a girl in despair, who fought loneliness, depression, and just about every other negative emotion those of the female persuasion struggle with. I wanted to die yet I wanted to live and, more than anything, I wanted to figure things out.

By the grace of God, I did. And now I hope to help you do the same.

Throughout the course of my grieving process, I learned two big lessons. One I'll share now and the other I'll save for later.

For now, here's the first: God loves me. It's simple and I've known it all my life yet I had to learn it in the context of my singleness. And what I learned was that His love for me is not proved or disproved by my relationship status. For much of my life I thought the fact I didn't have a husband meant God didn't love me as much as He did other women. Married women, to be specific. I not only felt abandoned and unwanted by men but also abandoned and unwanted by God.

This led to a decade-long grieving process. And though I eventually got to a place where the hope is stronger than the sorrow, it was a long, heartbreaking journey.

This is what I went through—every ache and tear, every moment when I wondered if I even wanted to wake up the next morning. But I did, and I'm the better for it. Now, I pray for you, hoping that by reading this you, too, can find healing.

And be able to tell a love story of your own.

The Beginning

Fireworks sparked and danced above my head that cool July night. I stood amidst strangers—thousands of them—on my first day as a resident of Colorado Springs. As I enjoyed the celebration one thought forced its way forward and tickled my brain.

"Maybe he's here. In this crowd. Looking for me like I'm looking for him."

I'd spent most of my adult life moving from state to state and town to town and job to job, until I eventually followed a dream to Colorado. When I arrived I didn't know a soul, except the nice woman at Woodmen Valley Chapel, which would soon become my church home, who helped me find a temporary place to live while I settled in and looked for a job. I didn't know what God had planned for me, living in the shadow of the Rocky Mountains, but I believed with all my heart that He'd led me West to meet the man He'd set aside just for me. And, perhaps, that man was in Memorial Park that Fourth of July, wondering if I was there too.

In case it's not obvious, I'm a bit of a romantic. I walked back to my apartment after the fireworks, full of hope. Then proceeded to spend the next several years job hunting, interviewing, moving again (and again and again), taking bits-and-pieces jobs until I finally found a good one, and, through it all, wondering where Park Man was and when we'd actually meet.

We didn't. That's probably apparent. But that didn't negate the fact that I had a dream I couldn't let go. It was a good dream, full of love and romance, a wedding and children and my own happily ever after. Best of all, I didn't have to pursue this particular dream. It's not like getting an education or establishing a career or writing a bestseller or climbing Mount Everest. Those dreams we chase. Marriage, I always believed, would just happen in God's time. But it's those last three words—in God's time—that are the most important, and the easiest to forget.

Anyway, back to the dream. Throughout my twenties and thirties I didn't worry about it. I made an effort not to be that girl who's marriage-crazy. You know, the one people describe as "desperate" or "pathetic," which only gets worse as you get older. That's when people start exchanging looks and shaking their heads and saying, "Bless her heart, she never did find a husband."

I tried to be patient. Waited for "him" to come to me. My mom told me to "chase him until he catches you" and that kind of stuck. Whatever that meant.

I understood he should think he did all the pursuing without actually knowing I was using my charms to lure him to me. Mom just never taught me how to use said charms in any way, let alone an alluring one. During my younger years, I had a crush on a guy every five minutes, and I did a lot of awkward, anonymous chasing. I even sent one boy flowers, complete with an appropriately cheesy sentiment.

God bless my high school heart. I honestly didn't have a clue.

As I got older, fortunately, I calmed down and tried to work on my patience. *When he comes along,* I convinced myself, *it will all come together in some great and mysterious way.* I would flirt and be cute and approachable and, suddenly, magically, say all the right things.

Boom. Love. Just like in a romance novel or on an episode of *The Love Boat*.

No one told me I would have to plan or fight or worry about falling in love. I focused all those energies and concerns on going to college and getting a job. Love would come. When I turned twenty-five as a single woman, it was no big deal. I had plenty of time.

Then I hit thirty. That was a bit of a surprise, but I chose to think optimistically. Much of my life was in turmoil, especially job- and where-will-I-live-wise. By then I had moved from Iowa to Michigan to New York to Vermont to Indiana, and I hadn't lived anywhere long enough to settle down and meet someone. I suppose if I had made a love connection I would have stayed, but I didn't. And, as I mentioned, I had confidence God wouldn't let me miss meeting my guy, no matter how many times I moved. I had faith.

But years rolled by and no one came along. Colorado

was as man-dry for me as all the previous states had been. Nothing had gone the way I always believed it would.

In my early forties, I met a man. *The man*, or so I thought. Mr. Right and Wonderful. Cute and charming and funny—I fell harder for him than any other guy before. The first time I saw him, I stumbled into a crush like a high schooler. We sat in a circle on a carpeted basement floor at a friend's house with about two dozen other singles, playing Catch Phrase, and he made me laugh. And if there's one thing I find irresistible, it's a man with a sense of humor.

After a few years of getting to know each other, we became friends and, for a moment in time, I thought we were moving toward something more. We flirted like teenagers, laughed at inside jokes, winked and smiled, and I touched his arm every chance I got. Even better, he touched mine.

Then I blinked and it was over. Like hitting a patch of ice in high heels, I was knocked down by the realization he wasn't into me after all, and I was trapped in the loss of something I never had. For months I had thought we were only one star-lit night away from our first kiss. When it became clear it had all been in my imagination, I could hardly bear it. How could I have been so wrong?

Even now, years later, it still makes me sad. I understand why things had to happen the way they did, but that doesn't make it any less painful.

Not long after this realization, I went to a friend's house for dinner. As I stood in Treshia's kitchen, watching her stir spaghetti sauce, I fought the tears I didn't feel comfortable sharing.

"He's not interested," I told her. It was over and my singleness stretched before me like a desert highway.

"Why can't I move past this?" I said, still trying to keep my emotions under control. "Why can't I just be single and happy and stop wanting more?"

Treshia tilted her head, studying me, as if she wasn't sure how much I could handle. Then she said, "You're grieving something you've lost, Sharyn. It's okay to be sad."

Isn't it funny how one moment can change how you look at your life? Well, maybe not ha-ha funny but certainly making-sense-of-the-ridiculous funny. In that one comment, I realized I wasn't just grieving the end of what I had hoped would be a love-relationship, I was grieving the potential loss of my dreams for marriage and a family of my own.

And deep down, the thought that maybe God didn't want me either shredded my confidence into pieces.

That day was the beginning of my journey through grief. For the first time, it hit me that my dream of marriage—the one I had never doubted would come true before—might, actually, go unfulfilled. And when a dream turns like that, it becomes more than a disappointment. It takes you to a place of grief. My friend was right. The possibility of never getting married went beyond everything I'd ever believed about my life.

So I did what any normal person would do. I ignored it. "I'm not sad," I told myself. "And I have plenty of time."

I ignored it when I was thirty-eight and my doctor told me it was already too late for me to have children.

I ignored it when I turned forty-five.

I ignored it when I moved away from my beloved, this-is-where-my-guy-lives Colorado, even more single than when I'd moved there almost a decade before.

And I tried to ignore it one night when God nudged my heart during a particularly grievous over-forty-and-still-single moment and said, "You should write about this."

I should write about this? Was He kidding? Why would I want to write about my deepest wound? No, thank you. Because the truth was, I was heavy-duty grieving by that point. I'd finally stopped ignoring it and accepted the struggle for what it was. It would hit me like a cyclone appearing suddenly out of nowhere—the pain of loneliness, or the depression of having two empty arms with no one to hold, and the knowledge that my ability to have children was dying a little more each day. As much as I wanted to remain hopeful, I'd been clinging to my dream of marriage for over three decades.

How much longer could I hold on? How much longer could I pretend I was fine? As I got older, the hurt turned to a gut-wrenching pain that came out of me in deep bursts of sorrow that I had no control over. I would shriek at the heavens and clench my fists and beg God to answer my prayer. I would have settled for any response ... but all I got was a hollow quiet.

Throughout the Psalms, the writers ask God to hear their prayers and to not be silent. Yet all I truly felt I heard from Him was, "Write about it."

How could He ask me to do that? How could He break my heart—deny me the one thing I'd always longed for—then tell me to put down on paper the grief and pain and sin that brokenness had led to?

My biggest argument against it was the fact that I didn't know what to say. The best I thought I could do was to write something along the lines of, "Um, yeah, being old and still single stinks. But hey, we can crawl through the trenches together, if you want."

I didn't have any answers. The last stage of grief is hope, and I wasn't there yet. I wasn't even close.

So I did what I'd been doing so easily for so long: I ignored the nudge to write about my situation and went on crying and grieving and pointing a finger at God for not stepping in and fixing it.

Of course, just because we've pushed something aside doesn't mean God has, right?

A few months later while at a writers' conference, I sat in on an editors' panel. At one point, they discussed what they were looking for in manuscript submissions. One of them actually said she wanted to see a book for older single women.

I admit it gave me a jolt. Because no matter how sad I felt, I was a writer and a writer knows the importance of diving into the nitty-gritty of her life. I began to brainstorm ideas and quickly came up with a concept: to take the seven stages of grief—denial, disbelief, bargaining, anger, guilt, depression, and hope—and explore how they relate to singleness. I kept notebooks by my bed where I could journal my thoughts.

But as I wrote, the thought that I still didn't have any answers continued to bother me. I was writing from a place of grief. How could I help anyone? It seemed crazy and stupid and, at the same time, like I was finally doing something I'd always been meant to do. I just needed to be vulnerable. As the saying goes, "Writing is easy. You just cut open a vein and bleed on the page." I bled so much it's a miracle I didn't go into shock.

Out of the grief came a story and out of the story came hope and out of the hope emerged a book. I titled it *Spinstered*.

Chapter 2

My So-called Single Life
Sweet Dreams

I grew up in Iowa, the second of five children. It was a good country life with two loving, godly parents. They raised my two brothers, two sisters, and me to know God and the Bible and to be a regular part of our local congregation. It's possible we were at our small-town community church more than the pastor's kids. Dad served as a deacon for as long as I can remember while Mom was involved in everything from leading the youth group choir to sign language interpreting for the deaf members.

We were also a creative family with interests in theatre, art, music, and writing. I wanted to be a writer from the time I wrote my first poem at the age of five.

And I wanted to fall in love. It sounded so wonderful, I couldn't wait for it to happen. I made up stories about true love and heroic men and perfect moments, and I've been writing about romance ever since. Seeing as I've never actually experienced it, though, I spend a lot of time praying my imagination won't fail me.

Still, what a strange turn of events. Why would God give me this longing, then withhold any opportunity to live it for myself? I had hints, moments when it seemed so close.

Like in the movie *Ladyhawke*, where the beautiful Isabeau was cursed to be a hawk during the day while her love, Navarre, turned into a wolf at night. And so they lived "always together, but eternally apart." Twice a day—at sunrise and sunset—they could almost touch. For that split second, they reached out for each other, yet couldn't quite make it. I've had moments like that, where I could almost touch something wonderful about to happen ... but it was just out of my grasp.

My dreams didn't help. Sometimes they were so real I would wake up absolutely certain *he* was close and as soon as I saw him, I would recognize him. For some reason, I always imagined him wearing flannel and smelling like leather and soap. We'd meet and, in that magical, true love way, just know it was meant to be. For so long I couldn't let that dream go. And I hated myself for it.

All of which brings me back to the question I asked my friend: Why couldn't I move on?

Broken

Remember Mr. not-so-Wonderful? The funny charmer I fell for who unwittingly broke my heart? Well, that wasn't the only way my life fell apart at the time.

When I lived in Colorado I had a great job—a dream job. I was content and hopeful. If things had worked out with Mr. W, it would have made for a perfect happy ending. People, myself included, would have said, "See? You just needed to be content with yourself before God could send the right guy into your life." But, as Orson Welles said, "If you want a happy ending, that depends, of course, on where you stop your story."

One Friday afternoon, I met Mr. W for lunch. I arrived at the restaurant first and heard him humming as he sauntered up behind me. It felt like my heart did a few somersaults before skipping around the room. I have no idea what we talked about, but I was happy. Since I had walked to the restaurant, he drove me back to my office. When I jumped out of his truck, my little white skirt flipped up in this flirty way that I couldn't have done on purpose if I had tried. He gave me a look that made me feel cute and desirable and I knew we were on our way.

"Soon," I thought. "He'll ask me out any day now."

At that same time, my company was downsizing, but I believed my job was safe. Turned out, I was wrong on both counts. The following Tuesday, my team gathered for devotions and a quick update. Someone suggested we pray for those in our department who would be laid off.

I didn't know we were praying for me.

Later that morning, I got an email saying my boss's boss wanted to meet with me at two that afternoon. It seemed strange so, being the worry wart I am, I stopped by her office to see what she wanted to talk to me about. This woman didn't ask to meet with me very often, but I wanted to believe she made an exception to discuss a new project or the dress code or something innocuous. Again, I was wrong. Really, really wrong.

Fifteen minutes later I had shut down my computer, grabbed a few personal items, and bolted out the door as fast as I could, hoping no one would see the tears I couldn't stop. My ideal, idyllic world crashed down around me, just like that. Even today, years later, memories of that moment—and the struggles afterward—still occasionally haunt me. Life went from relatively great to precariously uncertain. In a blink, I lost my financial security, small though it was. For months I tried, unsuccessfully, to find another job.

And all the hope I'd had for Mr. W disintegrated into

the realization that, in the end, he didn't want me. To this day, I still don't think I imagined everything I believed about the two of us, but it doesn't matter. He chose someone else.

I suppose that's obvious since it's been over a decade and I'm writing a book about being single.

Eventually, I ran out of options, so I sold my home and moved to Ohio. It seemed the best place since I had family there and I'd often thought it would be nice to be closer to my sister and nieces. When everything I did to try to stay in Colorado failed, I headed toward a new phase of my life.

Did I hope, maybe, my future husband was waiting for me in the Buckeye State? Oh, yes, I did. Boy, do I wish I would stop doing that.

Anyway, almost another year went by before I finally got a good job, which was about an hour from my family. I decided to split the difference and rented an apartment in a small town halfway between the two. I found myself in a new job, in a new town, no friends yet but, at least, I had family close by.

As it turned out, though, my apartment choice wasn't as brilliant as I thought. Instead, I felt isolated and vulnerable. The situation being what it was, 95 percent of the people I knew through work were married, which left me with few options for socializing. I felt so single that the idea of meeting someone not only seemed unlikely, it seemed impossible.

Why am I telling you this? To point out how God maneuvered me into a specific set of circumstances and then, around the same time, nudged me to write about being single over forty. It was rough, but, looking back, the timing was critical. I couldn't have written this book when

I felt successful, with a close, like-minded group of friends, in a situation where I knew at least a few available men I could imagine as possibilities.

Into this lonely world He dropped me, then asked me to write about my life as a single woman. A world where I felt completely off-kilter, lonely and lost. A world where I had to come face-to-face with the grief of what I'd missed because of time.

Why would He do that? Wouldn't it make more sense for me to delve into spinsterhood when everything was great? Why wait until I'm forlorn, sad, and more confused than ever?

Maybe because He didn't want me to write about the joys of singleness. I don't think we need another book about how to make the most of the situation or, even, how to get a man. Which I don't have a clue about anyway. Maybe I needed to be hyper-aware of all the negative aspects. To be at a place where I could say, "I know how hard it is. I understand the pain because I've been there."

How It Feels

He who has a "why" to live can bear with almost any "how."
—Friedrich Nietzche

The film *Frankie and Johnnie* starts with Michelle Pfieffer's character, Frankie, visiting her family. We quickly learn she's single and desperately lonely. Her mother wants to help, her heart breaking for her daughter. With a sigh, Frankie says, "I may not be the happiest person in the world, Mom, but it's not your fault." The next scene shows her sitting on a bus, headed home, her head pressed against the window, fingers swiping at the tears sliding down her cheeks.

That scene was so real to me because I'd been there. I knew the feel of the cold glass against my forehead, the scratchy heat of the seat, and the constant awareness of the hole boring through my heart. I had shed those tears. Over and over and over again. Always alone. Always wondering if God cared.

During this time, one verse in particular spoke to me in my grief: Psalm 56:8—"You number my wanderings; put my tears into your bottle; are they not in your book?"

I love this verse as a writer because I think it's beautifully poetic. But from my single perspective I wondered just how big that bottle is and where He kept it. Did God put my tears in that blue Depression glass bottle—in my mind it's always blue Depression glass—and then forget about it? A bottle is easily dismissed; a book is just as quickly put back on the shelf and forgotten.

Yes, I have a tendency to over-think things. I've done this with relationships more times than I can count. But I think the story of this verse is actually very simple. It tells me God is aware of every place I go … and He is doubly aware of every tear I cry. He collects them and keeps an ongoing tally.

I have a feeling God's collection of books containing the tears of single women could fill the Library of Congress a hundred times over.

Crying is perfectly natural for someone who's grieving. But unlike the grief we go through following a death, this singleness grief doesn't have a starting point. It's messier than that.

This book, for instance, has some order to it. I set up my chapters according to the seven stages of grief that I mentioned earlier. But I didn't write it in that order. I hopped around from one stage to another, journaling my thoughts and fears and joys and epiphanies, much like all the emotions hopping around inside of me. Regardless of the topic, you'll probably know when I was in a good mood and when I wasn't. The truly astute will even be able to determine when I was PMS-ing.

All that to say, we will not serenely wind our way through a charming little fairytale land called Spinsterville. It will feel more like a rollercoaster. Or a hurricane. Or a rollercoaster in a hurricane. At least, that's how it felt to me. But if, in the end, you find a reason for your grief, maybe you, too, can get off the ride and out of the storm.

First, though, we have to deal with regret. If grief is a monster then regret is the meat that sustains it.

If Only...

As I wrote and researched and thought about all that single over forty was and is and could be, it became clear that regret is the king of grief. "You should have tried harder, dreamed bigger, risked more." Regret crouches like a devil on my shoulder. If we're going to tackle grief, we need to charge head-on into regret.

My mom succumbed to breast cancer when I was a senior in high school, something a girl never forgets and never stops grieving. In this grief process, I am often, even more than thirty years later, overwhelmed by regret. I should have spent more time with her, asked her more questions and sat by her bed, listening to her share her life story slowly enough for me to write down every word. I regret everything I lost the day she died.

A few months before her cancer took its final turn for the worse, Mom came into our sunroom and sat down next to me as I played the piano. I don't remember what we talked about, but at some point she started crying.

"I'll never see you get married," she said. "I'll never meet my grandchildren."

To this day, I can only imagine how those remarks affected my life. At the time I didn't know she was dying—and wouldn't have believed it could happen if someone had told me it was possible—so I just thought she was being melodramatic. On that sunny, summer day, scented by fresh-flower breezes drifting through open windows, I assured her she was wrong. Everything would be fine. Then I changed the subject.

But she was right and by Christmas she was gone. Regret ate at me for years, often manifesting itself into dreams where I would have one more chance to talk to her, just a few more days to be a girl with her mom. In the midst of the grief, though, I had hope and still do. My mom loved her Savior, and I will see her again.

The regrets I've had as a single woman aren't much different in that they focus on what I didn't do. Could I have flirted more? Should I have dated the cabinet maker longer? Taken a chance on the unemployed guy ten years my junior whom I met on a plane? What about the one who said he would go out with me if I ever asked him? (Boy, that's just what a girl wants to hear.)

It's hard, if not impossible, to know if I could have done anything to change my current situation and what that should have been. All I can do is speculate. And what would be the point in that? It's in the past. I could live with the frustration … or choose to let it go and move on.

I could also learn from this and change my approach.

Say "yes" more, regardless of age or occupation, and be open to any Guy With Potential, or GWP as I like to call them, even when I don't feel a spark or am uncertain about any possible compatibility. I can take those risks while still having a clear idea of what I'm looking for and what would be good for me.

Here's the thing, though: I'm now past fifty and my looks aren't what they used to be. Single, available men even remotely close to my age are almost impossible to find. At this time, I don't have any GWPs in my social circle. A circle that is, sadly, pretty small. That doesn't mean one couldn't come into my life tomorrow, but I'm trying to be realistic.

It's very possible I "waited" too long and missed my chance. This is why I tell my story. Maybe someone could learn from my mistakes and not make the same ones. Call me a cautionary tale.

Of course, I'd much rather be the girl people point at and whisper, "She didn't meet the love of her life until later but, if you ask, she'll tell you she's glad she waited."

But that hasn't happened yet.

To get past regret is to remember and learn and change and never stop hoping. That's been a big answer to my prayers—I can be content single and still hope God has marriage in my future.

I didn't always feel that way. In fact, I used to hate it when people would throw the Philippians contentment verse* at me, as if that was supposed to make everything better and magically take away the pain. They didn't understand and neither did I. All I knew was my heart hurt and demanding I just "be content" wouldn't change that.

I needed to find a way to hope again. Not in a man or a husband or even a great job, but in something more. And though I knew "more" related to my relationship with God, it still took time for me to put it all together.

Never Too Late

After Mom died, I struggled with the loss for years as I worked through the stages of grief before finally reaching a place of acceptance and hope.

In grieving my single state, though, I felt relentlessly pulled away from hope, as each day my skin sagged a little more, I noticed more wrinkles or gray hairs, and the physical possibility of my ever having children of my own became less and less realistic. It became harder to convince myself that these particular dreams could still come true. In truth, it still is. I may be a self-titled Queen of Romance but even I have a hard time imagining a scenario where I will meet someone and fall in love. I'm not saying it can't happen but I no longer live in the daydream that it will.

And let's be honest—it's already too late for some of those dreams. I'll never know what it's like to be in love as a pretty, naïve young girl. My twenties and thirties skittered by without a proposal or even a decent kiss.

Now I look back on my forties and realize I'm slower, rougher around the edges, less trusting, and more quick to cry.

On the other hand, I still write poetry, am a sucker for a good romantic novel or Jane Austen movie, and sigh deeply whenever I hear Peter Gabriel's "In Your Eyes."

As the character Joan Wilder said in the movie *Romancing the Stone*,

"Hopeless romantic? Oh no. Hopeful. Hopeful romantic."

So I begin with hope, plan to end with hope, and have every intention of sprinkling it throughout this book. Because to grieve anything without hope is to grieve without God. Spinstered I may be, but I am hardly alone.

And neither are you.

---

*   "Not that I am speaking of being in need, for I have learned in whatever situation I am to be content" (Phil. 4:11).

Now, It's Your Turn

Writing my way through this has done me a world of good and I think it could be just as cathartic for you. So, I would like to encourage you to find yourself a journal in which to write down your own thoughts and reflections. I recommend you buy something new and pretty rather than any old notebook you found lying around. Just to make it more special.

At the end of each chapter, I'll offer a few suggestions to get you started, or you can write whatever is on your heart. Here are a few questions for Chapter 1:

- What are some of your childhood dreams? Which ones have you seen fulfilled? Which ones have you not? How do you feel about those dreams now?

- Have you given up on the possibility of marriage? Why or why not?

- Work through some events in your life that have led to your current attitude about being single. Should you have handled things differently? Is it something you can fix now?

- I mentioned Psalm 56:8 as a verse that I relate to my situation. Is there a Bible verse that speaks to you as a single woman? What is it about the verse that comforts or helps you?

Chapter 3

Denial
I'm All Right

Do not be in a hurry, the right man will come at last.
—Jane Austen, *Pride and Prejudice*

Some days I just don't know how to wrap my brain around the truth of my life. At times I can shrug and insist I'm fine walking this journey alone. What difference does it make? One path is as good as another. The next minute it feels so completely wrong. This isn't my life. I'm supposed to be married with children, like practically everyone I know. Being single is the illusion.

You know those movies where the main character hits her head or makes a wish or puts on a pair of pink bedazzled shoes and wakes up to find herself living a completely different life? That's me. Let's say I was in a car accident. As my body lies mangled and tube-attached in a hospital bed, I dream I have a chance to find out what it's really like to be single, a magical opportunity to learn to appreciate my husband and kids more. Someday I'll wake up from this illusion and find a strong arm around me as sweet, towheaded mini-mes bounce on the bed. Just like it's supposed to be.

But life isn't a movie. I'm living my reality. I don't know, though, when that moment was, that day—if there was a specific one—when I made the decision that landed me so firmly in Spinsterville. Did some great guy ask me out and I turned him down? Was someone interested but I never knew and, as a result, never gave him the encouragement he needed? Or was it a series of little things that ruined my chances—things I didn't even notice?

On the other hand, maybe there was nothing I could have done, no choice I could have made that would have resulted in marriage for me. But which is sadder: That I missed my opportunity, or I never had one? Instead of answering that question, I simply didn't let myself think about it.

Just remember God is in control and if He wanted you married, you'd be married. Let it go. Move on.

Ping-ponging back and forth between trying to convince myself it could still happen and feeling certain it never would seemed almost constant during my forties. But I couldn't stop clinging to hope, certain that if I made the right choices and tried harder, something would happen. It had to. I wasn't that old, yet. I wasn't unattractive or stuck in my ways. I was fun and interesting and passionate. At least, that's what I told myself. And, some days, I believed it.

I apologize for how negative that sounds but I have struggled with low self-esteem for most of my life. I'm not sure if I have low self-esteem because of my lack of any kind of a dating life, or I haven't had much of a dating life because of my low self-esteem. Probably a little of both. Kind of similar to the too picky/not good enough conundrum that I'll write more about in chapter four.

My friends and family have been supportive and happy-hopeful for me as I waited for a husband. I clung to their heartfelt reassurances that "somewhere out there is a fantastic guy that God has saved just for you. And we can't wait to see what happens when you meet him!" I occasionally felt encouraged when I heard that, seeing it as a word of hope from God.

The rest of the time it was more like a tiny thorn, pricking at my frustrated dreams. I had to remind myself that, though it sounded nice, no one but God knew if it was true or not. I grabbed onto optimism with both hands, saving pictures of wedding dresses and imagining long walks and whispered promises and sweet kisses at the front door. Still, as they say, wishing doesn't make it so, and, over the years, I felt the dream fading. I clung to it, desperately, unable to comprehend my life without true love in it and certain God wouldn't let me down in this respect.

Looking back, I see how easy it was for me to be selfish. The longer I went without a boyfriend, the more I felt I was getting a bum deal. I spent so much time thinking about my disappointments I rarely considered the needs and hurts and struggles of others. Some days, I even managed to convince myself their situation wasn't that bad. They didn't know what it was like. How could they?

It's hard to empathize when you're in denial.

Quality Alone Time

One Memorial Day weekend in my mid-forties, I found myself with nothing to do. Let me rephrase: I had no one to do something with. My family was out of town and I hadn't yet made friends in the area I'd moved to eight months prior. I knew a few single people, but, well, just because we were all husband-less didn't mean we'd naturally get along. Just like that I faced a long and, unless something happened, lonely weekend. Lonely to the point where, yes, the question as to just what my purpose on this planet could possibly be once again journeyed through my mind. My imagination often turned to the melodramatic in times of grief. It still can, to be honest, thanks to my theatrical background.

Anyway, I dreaded the thought of spending three days in relative isolation, so I tried to subtly hint that I was open to an invitation when my co-workers were discussing their weekend plans. Ridiculous, I know, considering they all came in twos and had families and busy lives. But that's how much I wanted to have plans.

I've seen similar reactions throughout my single life— a need to have options, even if I turned them down. Many single women struggle with the feeling that no one wants them and I imagine I'm not the only one who has wavered between staying home alone because she didn't want anyone to know her situation and just flat-out saying something in the hope it might lead to an invite.

This time, I spoke up. But no invitation came and that's when I whimpered into survivor mode for anyone who asked how I planned to spend the holiday.

"Oh, nothing special. But it's for the best."

I tried to say it like a normal person, forcing the corners of my mouth upward. It didn't work because then I'd gush into a laundry list of weekend activities.

"Really, I want to work on my novel, clean my car, do the dishes, maybe paint ... something. I can sure get a lot done in three days without any commitments!" (Cue dramatic background music.)

I don't know if they believed me, or just felt too sorry for me to say anything. What was I thinking anyway? I didn't want to go to someone's family gathering any more than they wanted me there. And I certainly didn't want a pity invite. That did happen once, several years before. One Thanksgiving while at a new job I had to work the next day, so I couldn't make it home for turkey and stuffing. A girl I barely knew from church invited me to join her family. The day was awkward and weird, but I suppose it could have been worse. Still, not something I would want to do again.

Anyway, back to Memorial Day weekend and me in denial. "I'm fine being alone. It's not the first time and it won't be the last. It's really no big deal."

And a single tear drips free and splashes on the TV remote.

Isn't it easy to convince yourself everything is grand and ignore the ache? It's something we simply get used to as the years rumble past. And the thing is, I *am* fine alone. I'm used to it. But there are times I wish it was more of a choice than the norm.

Thinking Outside the Box

A large box sits in my garage. Filled with papers, letters, poems, and various other items from years gone by, it's the box that travels from one storage room to another every time I move. A couple years ago I finally went through it, trying to decide what should stay and what should go. Which memories should I treasure and which should I forget?

It's not just a question about the box. And I probably kept more than I should have.

That old box, you see, contains remnants of my shattered, hopeful heart. Somewhere near the bottom is a faded "I love you" card I bought several decades ago, certain I would one day give it to my guy. The inside sentiment—"And to think we almost never met"—becomes more poignant and ironic with each passing year.

Poems I wrote expressing my hopes, frustrations, fears, and longings are stacked near the bottom. It even contains a few pictures of wedding dresses I collected during a time when I believed meeting someone, falling in love, and getting married would be the natural progression of my life and it could happen at any moment so I should be prepared. I thought it would be healthy evidence of positive thinking if I planned ahead. Heck, I knew women who *bought* their wedding dress before they even met the guy! Why couldn't I hang on to a few pictures?

So many dreams, all packed away in a beat-up, well-traveled cardboard box. Abandoned ... but not forgotten. Much like my heart. I spent most of my time purposefully *not* thinking about what I desired, trying to ignore the ache. Not planning, not hoping, not cutting out pictures or penning romantic sonnets about candles and chocolate hearts and the caress of fingers across my skin.

I pushed my heart into its own little box, taped it shut, and put it in its place. It was better that way. I could not swim in grief on a daily basis. Too many years had passed, and things just weren't the same. Continuing to hope for "someday" seemed so pointless.

Maybe tomorrow I'll deal with the box, but for now the dreams are right where they need to be.

Weathering the Storm

Maybe I'm strange but I actually love winter. I know, for many, it's a time when gloomy, cloudy, chilly days steal joy and, sometimes, lead to depression. I might feel that a bit in January and February, but it's not as bad as what so many of my friends go through. I've heard several mention how much they hate winter and how they see it as something to survive. They'd sleep through it if they could, but since they can't, all they can do is dream of warmer days.

For the most part, though, wintry weather and cloud-covered skies don't bother me. Yes, I look forward to spring, and I love sunlight. As soon as Daylight Saving Time hits, I start longing for open windows and fresh breezes to clear out the stale, trapped air.

But I love good storms too. There's something cozy and homey about rainy or snowy days. I kind of like being able to blame the weather for my decision *not* to go somewhere.

About a decade ago, I lived in Colorado, where it averages about two hundred and fifty sunny days a year. I don't know that I was happier. Maybe. The problem is I learned to put my emotions in a box. I trained myself not to feel. At least, not to feel anything too strong. I especially made regular choices to ignore any feelings of loneliness.

Every once in a while as I crawl into bed, I wonder why I still live by myself, and if it will always be this way. A wave of grief hits me, then I push the question aside.

There is no answer so why sob into my pillow? I'll sleep now and deal with this tomorrow.

Tomorrow, of course, never comes.

In my novel, *Spinstered*, Catie states, "I am more single today than I've ever been." I wrote that line in 2012 ... and it seems just as true today. Except now I can shrug as I say it. *Well, it is what it is.*

I don't know that this is better, but I do believe it's all

part of the process of singleness. And there is a light. It's dim and distant but it's coming my way. One cloudy day at a time.

It's Complicated

Okay, yes, I knew it was Valentine's Day. And, unlike some singles, the holiday doesn't, for the most part, bother me. To be honest, I've never been in a relationship on February 14, so over the years the day has simply become an opportunity to celebrate my love for family and friends. And I just ignore all that stuff about softly lit fondue dinners and passionate kisses.

This particular V-Day afternoon, as I headed to a quarterly all-staff meeting, my thoughts were focused on the writing project I'd been brainstorming, not fiancées and husbands and long-term love. I thought the heart-shaped snack cakes and cookies they offered us to munch on were cute, chocolate, and tasty. Grabbing a couple confections and a bottle of water, I took a seat near a few co-workers as the meeting started.

A woman stood and told us we would kick things off with a game. She began asking questions. "Who's been married the longest?" People yelled out numbers until we had a winner at forty-seven years.

That was just the beginning.

"Who's our most recent newlywed?"

"Who got engaged on Valentine's Day?"

"Who is celebrating their anniversary today?"

And on … and on … and on. I was fine, at first. But with each question, something dug just a little deeper and a little sharper. I looked around and realized I was one of about a handful of single people in the room. We were surrounded by wedding rings. The smile on my face slowly melted as I fought to hang on to my good mood or, at least, look that way. But after about ten minutes of this, I was done. I turned to the girl next to me and whispered, "This is brutal. I'm going to the bathroom."

The fun continued around me as I weaved my way through the rows of people, across the back of the room, out the door, down the hall, and into the nearest ladies room. I took refuge in the stall farthest from the entrance, where I turned and grasped the coat hook with both hands, trying to keep the crying as muted as possible. No one wants to hear someone weeping in the restroom. Besides, it was my pain, and I didn't want to have to explain myself to anyone. But it was too hard and, before I could stop it, a dry, broken sob escaped. If anyone heard it, though, they didn't say anything. After a few minutes, I regained my composure, dried my tears, checked my mascara, and returned to the meeting.

I never know when that pain wave will hit or how bad it will be or how long it will last. Some days, my married-with-children friends can talk about school projects and runny noses and how many times they had sex that week and I'm fine. Other days the mere mention of Dora lunch boxes or joint checking accounts makes me want to leap off the top of a very tall building.

Neverland

I think my favorite movies are the ones that remind me of a time in my life when I followed hope around like a lost puppy. I could name several 1980s and 90s flicks that immediately take me back to the dreamer I once was, from *Romancing the Stone* and *A Room With a View* to *You've Got Mail*, *While You Were Sleeping*, and *Only You*. I loved these movies then because I believed someday that spark, that kiss, that great love would happen to me.

Watching them now is a bittersweet experience. If only I could travel back in time and find that girl, tap her on the shoulder, and say, "Don't waste your daydreams and heartfelt sighs. It's just not gonna happen."

But then, it's probably best she didn't know then what I know now.

Films rarely have the same effect today. I'm not sure if it's because the movies are less romantic or I'm more jaded. I'm definitely more cynical. *I don't need a man. I don't need love. I'm fine just the way I am.* These words tremble with a power I don't necessarily feel. Yet I say them anyway.

Deep down, I will always be a dreamer. No matter what I do or how much I try to ignore it, I cannot escape my floaty, happy imagination. I have created scenarios where I meet the love of my life in ways that rival the best chick flicks around. He shows up when I need him most, asks me to dance when it seemed no one would, kisses me just right as we stand hand-in-hand on a snow-covered lane. In my mind, our conversations are always clever, our attraction instantaneous. This is my dream world, or was. I really don't visit it as often as I used to.

It's that whole boxed-up emotions thing.

Even today, as I face an uncertain future, I can imagine wonderful outcomes—a great job, a bestseller, some fun, new beginning that takes me completely by surprise. And each dream leads to Mr. Right. In fact, almost every daydream I've had ended with a kiss, perhaps a ring. Just like a good romantic movie should. If only wishing made it so.

I have to accept the fact that it's quite possible none of these wishes will be fulfilled. As much as I'd like to believe otherwise, romantic possibilities are a lot harder to find as you get older. That's why love stories, more often than not, feature young, beautiful people. I sometimes feel foolish to think that—after all these years—suddenly someone will come along who wants the same dream ... with me.

For most of my life, every Christmas I would think, "Maybe next year I'll be in a relationship." It always happened right around the holidays. That's when I most wanted someone in my life. Twenty, fifteen, even ten years ago, I looked into my future with confidence, believing there was no way I'd reach my forties without a wedding ring. But I continued to age and, as I did, I began to see years of singleness stretching in front of me.

I wish I could deny it, but I can't.

Denial, sadly, kept me in a place outside of reality. And whenever I told myself to snap out of it, I realized how tired I was. Tired of feeling unattractive and dull. Tired of worrying about money and my weight and whether or not I'm appealing to men. Tired of being afraid. Tired of the almost constant sense of dread. And tired of feeling insecure and unsafe.

Yes, as I wrote this section I was sad. A common feeling during the grief process, of course. By the grace of God, though, I forged my way out of the pit of despair, knowing He held my hand all the way through the valley. I remembered His unfailing love and mercy toward me and could rejoice in the future He has in store.

But in that moment I was grieving, and all I could do was ask my Savior to pull me through.

Things Unseen

Years ago—so long ago, in fact, that I only remember a few details—I wrote a humorous little ditty to sing at a friend's bridal shower. It talked about the changes she would have to make as a wife and some of the benefits of being single that she would soon miss out on. The only line I remember is, "Does this mean you'll have to shave your legs now?"

Sure, I hoped it would merit a few laughs, but I also thought it was a legitimate, if silly, question. I've gotten used to the fact that no one knows or cares if my legs look a bit Yeti-like in the throes of deep winter. Though I certainly care about personal hygiene and my appearance, it's surprisingly easy, as time passes, to let go of some of those things that aren't noticeable.

For instance, why should I spend money on fancy new underwear when what I have is perfectly serviceable? And by "perfectly serviceable," I mean not falling apart and performing its rightful function. Which also means that, while I might plunk down forty bucks for boyfriend pants at *Victoria's Secret*, the only store that usually sees my underclothing money starts with a "W" and ends with a "Mart." If no one else cares, I tell myself, why should I?

It's easy to convince myself it doesn't matter. It's not so easy to ignore that little voice that asks, "But what if it does?" What if this laissez faire attitude comes across to the men I meet, even if they can't actually put it into words? And it's not only in the area of romantic relationships. It is, quite possibly, why I've had such a hard time holding onto a job. Even when I had a position I loved, something stopped me from being wholly committed. It's certainly kept me from losing weight. I'm only just beginning to realize how much I've held myself back, and how I've been my own worst enemy.

My sister, Kris, told me as much once. It was a few weeks before Christmas, and she mentioned plans to get a pedicure. I shrugged the idea off, commenting, "What's the point? No one will see my feet until spring."

She replied, "It's that kind of attitude that keeps you single."

The comment made me stop and think. Though Kris and I don't agree on a lot of things, I can appreciate her insight. It would be foolish not to pay attention. So I have to ask myself if it's true. Does my attitude about how I present myself encourage men to look elsewhere?

In the first chapter, I mentioned a piece of art I like—a lovely pastel print of a young girl holding a glass jar. Next to the picture is Psalm 56:8—"You number my wanderings; put my tears into Your bottle; are they not in Your book?" I not only thought it was pretty, but it expressed my hope that God cares about my pain.

During one of my moves into a new apartment, I had all my art sitting out while I tried to determine where to hang everything. My sisters had stopped by to help me decorate. Kris noticed this particular print and said, "You need to get rid of that."

"What? Why? I love it! It's one of my favorites."

"Because," she replied, "you're letting it define you." Kris, by the way, studied psychology in college.

My youngest sister, Susie, chimed in. "She's right. Let it go."

Yep, those are my sisters for you. Straightforward. Yet although they speak their minds, they don't push. I looked from one to the other, trying to think of a good argument in the face of such sound reasoning, and finally whimpered, "But I like it."

"Then keep it," Kris said with a shrug.

Like I said, straightforward.

She continued, "But at least put it somewhere no one can see it. You don't want guys to know you feel that way." Well, I couldn't argue with that and the print has been in storage ever since.

In case you couldn't tell, my sisters are pretty good at showing me the signals I'm sending out, unwittingly. A few years ago, Susie went to a singles dance with me. Though she was married, she agreed to tag along for moral support since I didn't know many people in the area. We had a fun, if low-key, evening and I think she was a bit surprised by my, shall we say, difficulty interacting with men.

At one point, a guy asked me to dance. I was surprised and I'm sure it showed, which probably didn't help me. But I said yes and we danced and that was about it for me dancing with men that night ... even though the room was full of single guys. I did, however, rock the Electric Slide with the other wallflowers!

On the way home, Susie told me that when the man—who was someone I had met before—walked up to me, I crossed my arms and took a step back. It was done unconsciously but, I suppose, that's the problem.

Here we have another instance of the "I'm-a-mess, stay-away" vibe I send out, yet I still tell myself I'm not doing anything wrong. Obviously it's the fault of the men I meet. They don't try hard enough to get to know me or they're not attracted to me. And if I don't blame men, I blame God. It's certainly easier to be the victim.

Still, if I'm sending out an attitude that screams, "Don't touch me! I'm not interested!" why should I be surprised when men pick up on that?

I get in my own way by not caring enough. By thinking no one else cares, so why should I? Other women do it by focusing on other things. You can give off a "Don't touch me! I'm not interested!" vibe by being overly busy and committed to your job. These are not bad things, but it's to our benefit to recognize the things we're doing that push men away. And then decide if we're okay with that.

My sisters and female friends have told me I can be rough on the opposite sex. The irony is that I see wives doing the same thing to their husbands, and it bothers me. I can recognize it in them but not in myself. I don't like thinking I'm mean or, heaven forbid, a harpy, yet I have to acknowledge that I've felt resentment toward men *because* they don't like me. Which sounds strange and stupid, but there it is. Though I've tried, I can't always keep it inside, and the anger comes out in sarcastic remarks and harsh comments. But more about that in chapter six.

Nevertheless, because I was in denial about my attitude, I didn't know how to connect with men, which probably didn't make me particularly attractive to them. Knowing they're not interested made me angry and, in that anger, I pushed them away. It was a vicious circle. One I've had a hard time escaping. Again, I had to decide if I wanted to change the things about me that got in the way of potential relationships.

Before it was too late.

To be honest, I'm not even sure I will know how to create a relationship with a man when I finally have the chance. I tell myself things will just come together with Mr. Right, and I won't have to worry about saying something stupid or having broccoli in my teeth. My issues and insecurities won't matter. Everything will flow like well-written dialog, perfectly scripted with unexpected passion, an instant connection, and a sense of humor. In fact, many of these "scenes" have ended up in my fiction writing. Maybe it won't be easy—who wants that?—but it will be natural.

Yeah, right. Wouldn't that be nice? If only my life was a Sandra Bullock rom-com.

Instead, I have a knack for putting my foot in my mouth and, at the same time, pushing men away. I'd like to think the love of my life would find all my issues and insecurities cute, even charming. That's how it works in Hollywood, right? It's more likely he'll think I'm weird and in need of medication.

As far as I can tell, men want quiet, complacent, sweet women who either love to exercise or can maintain a size two figure without it. They don't want loud, insecure, chunky chicks who speak their minds.

On the other hand, sometimes I'm so worried I'll say something ridiculous that I don't say anything at all. I have seen a look cross a man's face that says, to me anyway, "Wow, I could never be interested in her." I hate that look.

Most of the time, in any case I stumble in a race between my brain and my mouth. Boy, have I said some silly things! Fortunately, it's been years since a man made me so nervous I could barely speak. I guess I'm growing up and, well, not meeting very many eligible men.

In my youth, I fell for boys left and right. In my imagination, we would talk and laugh and I'd be so clever he couldn't help but fall right back. Then, inevitably, there he'd be in real life, standing in front of me, and those well-scripted words darted out of my head like a hummingbird. Just getting out a simple "hi" was a minor miracle.

Things improved as I got older because I became better at pushing insecurities aside and trusting my instincts a little more. I would *act* like the girl I wanted to be.

It didn't help. I would still say ridiculous, *what-on-earth-is-wrong-with-you* things that I would kick myself over for days after. I would share an example or two with you here but, thankfully, I seem to have pushed them out of my memory.

All this to say, I am on the other side of the world from women who are comfortable around men. They are like aliens to me. Life isn't scripted, to my everlasting disappointment, and it seems the only way I can have the kind of romantic conversation with my dream man is to write a play and cast myself as the lead, with Mr. Right as my love interest.

Hmm. That's not such a bad idea.

Anyway, all of this imperfectness brings us right back to The Single Woman Mantra: "My guy will love me just the way I am!"

Yes, of course he will. If God has a spouse in your future. I've read that, statistically, most of us will get married someday. But it's not a guarantee. I know that sounds awful gloomy and I hate writing it but, fortunately, this is only chapter two. Remember, this is a journey *toward* hope. And we're not there yet.

Story of Hope—Leasey

In my twenties I went to law school and fell in love with my best guy-friend. I was sure we would marry, but we broke up in the years after graduating. We remained friends, though, and both of us stayed single. Then I entered the world of work. I finally began to meet men and to go out with them. I felt so pretty and desirable for the first time in my life, that even though I was still single at thirty, I wasn't concerned. I enjoyed life too much.

I started to worry, though, as my thirties marched on. One day I looked around my church and saw many attractive, professional women who were older than me and still single. For the first time, I became truly alarmed that a lot of women might not get married. But I would. I still had guy friends, plus I was meeting new people and dating. And I was prayerfully trying to cultivate the heart of a wife so that I would be ready when my husband finally claimed me. This would happen soon, I was sure.

Then, a few months before I turned forty, my best guy-friend from law school shocked me with the news that he was getting married.

All I could think was, "Why did he want to marry this woman when he hadn't wanted to marry me?"

Another alarm bell sounded that maybe I wouldn't get married. I was shaken to the core.

My fortieth birthday arrived and I was still single. One of the worst things I had imagined throughout my twenties and thirties had happened. But my life was not the horrific, lonely disappointment I had feared.

So, to celebrate I threw myself a dinner party at an enchanting Italian restaurant in Manhattan. I dined in a fancy restaurant, which I was able to afford, surrounded by friends and family who loved me. I was in perfect health—and looked good, if I do say so myself.

And yes, I wished there was a man beside me.

But there was much in my life for which I was thankful. And being forty and single came with an unexpected gift: freedom. I was able to shrug off that heavy, burdensome thing—the search for the right man—that had been riding my back for so many years. What a relief!

My prayer began to be, "Okay, Lord, if marriage is not going to happen, then could I have a life that is so totally amazing that I wouldn't mind not having a husband?" And God's answer was, "Yes!"

Ultimately, I left the harrowing practice of law and relocated to go back to school, on a scholarship. I am studying theology and pursuing my call to ministry. It's my dream come true! I spent one summer in South Africa working with a church. I may teach somewhere when I am done with school, or lead a women's ministry, or (gasp!) pastor a church. I am asking the Lord to surprise me with something wonderful.

I am now mid-forties and single. I can't believe I will never get married. But I am not a hostage to singleness waiting for a husband to rescue me. There is life in my life! Each single year gets more and more full of goodness.

Leasey Brown
Divinity Student
Durham, NC

Now, It's Your Turn

- Which holidays are particularly hard for you as a single woman? How do you cope?

- Do you have dreams packed away in a cardboard box—or something similar—that you don't want to deal with? What are they? How do they make you feel now?

- Write about some movies that have impacted your life. Why did they affect you and how?

- Do you think you're in denial regarding your singleness? What are some things you've told yourself to feel better? Are they true? What do your answers tell you about yourself?

- What's your biggest challenge where men are concerned?

- Do you still believe God has someone for you? How does your answer—yes or no—make you feel?

Chapter 4

Disbelief
I Still Haven't Found What I'm Looking For

*Even in laughter the heart may sorrow,
And the end of mirth may be grief.*
—Proverbs 14:13

How am I still single? And at my age! People get married every day and I always believed that was a part of my future. Yet here I am, still singing solos in the shower. Actually, I think I'm in an almost constant state of disbelief. I certainly didn't plan or prepare for this. Women who long for marriage and family don't sit around in their twenties and map out how they'll handle singlehood in their forties.

For the first two and a half decades of my life I fully believed I would marry before I hit thirty, about the same age my mom was when she and Dad tied the knot. It made sense to me. Finish your education, figure out your career—to a certain degree anyway, get married, get pregnant, raise your family, etc.

I got a bit lost for a while in my twenties, roaming from one state to another and from one going-nowhere job to an even worse one. Still, my timeline seemed perfectly reasonable. The fact that I had not yet had any kind of serious boyfriend hardly seemed like something to worry about. I only needed one perfect guy—the one God had planned for me. Why waste my heart on someone who wasn't right? God would bring him into my life at the perfect time. Why *wouldn't* I believe that?

Today, almost thirty years later, people occasionally tell me there's someone really amazing out there for me. And it's what I tell myself, though with varying levels of certainty. Most days, though, it's hard to comprehend the facts of my singleness. I mean, I am *really* single. Any more single and I'd be a nun.

My sister, Susie, a professional photographer, needed religious stock photos and had me dress up in a nun's habit for the shoot. At one point, she said, "You know, you actually look pretty good."

I replied, "Well, it isn't that much of a leap." At that moment, she snapped the picture. The expression on my face made me laugh, so I set it up as my Facebook profile photo for a while. But so many people asked me if I had, in fact, taken the vows, I finally replaced it.

That's right. I'm so single people wouldn't be surprised to learn I'd decided to become a nun. Just shoot me now.

Anyway, as I write this there aren't any eligible, available, age-appropriate men in my life—and there hasn't been one for years. No one to flirt with or hope to see over the weekend or write silly poems about. The possibility of falling in love has never seemed so remote as it does right now. It's harder and harder to imagine it will ever happen.

And that's part of the problem. Disbelief strangles hope. If you cannot believe something different is possible, how can you hope things will change? Hope, by its very essence, requires belief.

The apostle James wrote: "But let him ask in faith, with no doubting, for the one who doubts is like a wave of the sea, driven and tossed by the wind" (1:6).

He's speaking, specifically, about praying for wisdom

here, but then he adds that stuff about doubting and how anyone who doubts should not suppose they will receive anything from the Lord. This certainly isn't the only time God lets us know how He feels about doubt. It is, after all, the opposite of faith.

Actions, Not Words

Sing me no song, read me no rhyme, don't waste my time. Show me! Don't talk of June, don't talk of fall, don't talk at all! Show me!
—Eliza Doolittle, *My Fair Lady*

On those rare occasions—alone in my room or driving home in my car, trapped in my grief—when I cried out my despair to God, I often wondered, for a brief moment, if He hated me. After that split second of insanity, though, I realized my true fear was not that He hated, but that He didn't care. They say apathy, not hate, is the opposite of love, and I believe it. When you hate someone at least you're still thinking about them. But apathy? Well, that's just out of sight, out of mind.

All I knew was it seemed I'd prayed the same prayer, cried the same tears, and begged for Him to answer so many times I felt foolish trying it yet again. In the end it just seemed pointless. *If He didn't do anything the previous nine hundred and ninety nine times, why should this prayer be any different?* It wasn't enough to know He was listening; I needed action. An arm around my shoulders and a quiet voice saying, "It will be all right." A whisper of love, protection ... hope.

Should I, like Elijah, hear that voice in a breeze weaving through my hair? Possibly. Should I see His love in a sunset or feel it in the cheery hugs and kisses of my nieces and nephews? Absolutely. Is it okay that sometimes that just isn't enough? I think so. Because in choosing to believe God loves me, I also must believe He cares and that this desire I have for a family is good and right and given to me by Him.

So, yes, I believe He loves me. But I have still spent decades waiting. Combine all these things and you get some serious frustration. I can wax poetic about breezes, hugs, and sunsets until tears come to my eyes—and don't doubt it for a minute, they often do—but this girl still feels she's missed out on something. From the simple things like wanting to hold hands and make out in the back seat of the car to wishing I had someone to laugh with, share dreams with and walk alongside, I want more.

Is that so wrong?

Twisting the Knife

The retreat had been a writer's dream. Three days of harvesting creativity and drawing closer to God while cozying up with other artists in a gorgeous lodge outside of Buena Vista, Colorado. Our time concluded with praise and tears and a renewed passion to put pen to paper. Even better, the final day of the retreat was my birthday, and I'd been surprised that morning with a waffle smothered in ice cream, whipped cream, chocolate sauce, and M&Ms. A lone pink candle floated on top of the messy concoction, waiting for me to blow it out with one quick, delighted breath.

A few hours later we were headed home, happy with what we had accomplished and talking about the dreams and ideas the weekend had birthed. I ended up carpooling with two middle-aged married women and a sixteen-year-old girl. We spent most of the more than two-hour journey discussing art and ways we planned to keep our creative spark ignited now that our lives were moving back to some semblance of normal.

Within a few miles of the parking lot in Colorado Springs where I'd left my car, the conversation turned to relationships, and I found myself telling them some of the frustrations I had with men. Nothing mean or judgmental, I merely shared an observation. Half joking but feeling a point should be made, I turned to the young girl sitting next to me and said, "If you ever want to get married, do it while you're young. Because the older you get, the harder it will be to find someone decent."

Suddenly, all hell broke loose, and I'm only mildly exaggerating. You would have thought I had suggested she get married the next day or, at the very least, give up every other dream she had ever had in lieu of marriage. The two older women threw their hands in the air with a collective gasp, the one driving practically swerved off the road, and the other turned her head so fast it nearly snapped off.

"Don't tell her that!" they exclaimed, as close to unison as a Milli Vanilli song. In that moment, I was the enemy of all women and this poor child was my innocent victim.

Their reaction stunned me into silence. Before I had a chance to say anything in my defense, one of the women turned to the girl and said, "Don't listen to her."

The child responded, "Why would I listen to her? She's forty and still single."

That moment still replays through my mind like a scene from a John Hughes movie. I'm the grown-up version of Samantha Baker, without Jake Ryan. How do you respond to something that mean? What started out as a perfectly fine discussion about art had, within minutes, turned into an incredibly painful attack on my heart. I don't think they meant to hurt me, but they sure did.

And the irony is that perhaps she might want to listen to me *because* I was forty and single. It's certainly ironic that these two married Christian women had seemingly fallen for the feminist nonsense telling us women should not want marriage.

Finally, it seems hugely ironic that they all decided I didn't know what I was talking about when I was, factually speaking, the only one in the car who did. Why would they be so quick to denounce marriage as something that shouldn't be pursued? Has feminism really taken us so far from God's ideal that we can no longer recognize the blessings connected to marriage and family?

Many of the happily wed cannot begin to understand, thinking we really do cherish total control of the remote (as if that's something to long for), believing we're so lucky to have so much free time and so few commitments. They dream about living even one day as a single woman, and I'm sure they would enjoy it.

But it wouldn't take long, would it? Eventually, the emptiness would hit and they'd realize how lonely they are, and how it feels to go weeks without any physical human contact, to know just how friendless and cold and uninspiring that remote is.

Just like that, they would hurry back to their homes, embrace their husband and children, and be reminded of the magic to be found in cuddling up next to the ones you love. Okay, yes, I have total control of what's on the TV, but it's also been three decades since someone's taken my hand in his. Do you really need to ask which I would choose if I could?

I'm still not entirely sure why those three females decided I didn't have a clue what I was talking about or why they chose to be so hurtful about it. But, dear God, it stung. It still stings. I do know something about the topic and it has led me to prayerful study of Scripture. I have wept and ached and agonized over this, and I've engaged in numerous conversations with other single women—and men, for that matter—throughout most of my life. Yet my years of experience and wisdom were dismissed.

Far worse, they were dismissed precisely for the very reason they were relevant.

That said, I can certainly understand why they didn't want to hear what I was saying. The girl was, well, merely a child and, as such, far too caught up in her life at the moment to give heed to a someday so far in the future it couldn't even begin to matter. But if she had been willing to listen and had been open enough to realize I did actually have some idea what I was talking about, I would have told her the next few years would skip past her like happy little children, so fast she would miss the smiles on their faces.

I would have told her not to be afraid, to risk getting hurt more, and to not hide or run away from possibilities. To never weigh herself or worry about what size she wears. To always believe she is beautiful enough to be loved and cherished. I might have warned her not to wait for her dreams to happen but to race after what she wants, seeking God's will as she does. To chase life down and drink it up. All the things I wish someone would have told me when I was sixteen. My advice may not have had any impact on this particular girl, but now we'll never know.

For their part, I suppose the married women, for one,

didn't want to hear that the fantasy they imagined as the single life simply isn't all it's cracked up to be and, two, it's possible they really believe career matters more than relationships. They certainly felt strongly about sixteen-year-old girls not giving any thought to their future as it relates to marriage and family. Career, sure. College, definitely. Finding a husband? Certainly not! But who really knows what motivated them to react as they did. They seemed more interested in quieting me than they were in discussing the issue.

I suspect all they heard were the disappointed hopes of a lonely, single woman who, in their minds, was trying to convince some high school girl that her highest goal in life should be to live barefoot and pregnant. Heaven forbid.

All I know is that after I'm gone, it's the loved ones I leave behind who will remember me and, potentially, offer a legacy to my life, not the reports I wrote or the meetings I attended. A good career is fun and empowering and a great blessing if you can find one you enjoy, but it's one of those temporary things the Bible talks about. Few jobs still have meaning after you retire. Your dream employer will just find someone else to take your place. Or, as in my case of being laid off twice, they'll simply discover they never really needed you anyway.

Perhaps it was short-sighted naiveté that attacked me in the car that day. When we get caught up in the superficial accolades of the moment, it can be easy to forget the meaning your life could have long-term. Society has stood on the foundation of family for thousands of years, yet now we move into these "enlightened" times and we're suddenly supposed to tow the feminist line and deny our desire for marriage and kids?

I can't do it. And I feel that by not caving to these ideas I give myself permission to grieve what I've lost so far and to believe it's okay to want and hope for a family. Even when I don't have answers. Even when I'm treated as foolish. Even when that spinstered box they have put me in is an abandoned, painful one.

At Least She Has a Good Personality

There will be little rubs and disappointments everywhere, and we are all apt to expect too much; but then, if one scheme of happiness fails, human nature turns to another; if the first calculation is wrong, we make a second better: we find comfort somewhere.
—Jane Austen, *Mansfield Park*

I'm not beautiful. Let's just say it. Still, I do have a few good qualities—dark blue eyes, naturally blonde hair, and surprisingly cute feet. No, really! Anyway, I'm also thirty-some pounds overweight and the years are starting to show. My German and Norwegian genes, fortunately, help me look younger than my age ... but have little impact on how I feel.

Just as I was starting to like and accept myself "as is," I came to realize I had, without noticing, wandered past my prime. Not that my prime was much to sing about considering the fact I never truly took advantage of it, relationship-wise. Somehow, I missed out on romance during the healthiest, tightest-skinned years of my life. I was unable to make something significant happen with any of the eligible men I met in my younger years. Now I am in the unenviable position of trying to attract someone with, well, whatever's left.

I know that sounds uber-negative. Friends and family tell me I'm pretty and they mean it. Their compliments encourage me and I appreciate them. But I also see how men don't notice me. They just don't. Most walk by me without a glance. This is a fact of my life, and I won't sugarcoat it to make myself feel better.

A few years ago I had moved to a new state and started a new job and decided I needed a new haircut to go along with it. Naturally, all of these changes inspired in me a hope of potentially meeting someone. Why not go for it and actually pay a pretty penny for a pretty and different look? One of my co-workers recommended a specific stylist at a nearby salon, so I made an appointment.

Maybe I shouldn't have had such high expectations, but I was excited to see what this guy could do. I typically don't like to give a hairstylist too much direction since she—or he, in this particular case—is the professional. Maybe I'll offer a few suggestions. Still, I dream of the day when the stylist says, in a sexy French accent, "Zis is ze perfect look for your face shape and style and personalitee. You are going to love eet!" Sadly, that's never happened.

I told him the basics of what I wanted—a few highlights and an easy-to-style, flowy cut that would frame my face. I'd had highlights before and always liked how it looked, feeling the streaks of pale gold made my skin brighter and my eyes a little bluer. But because my hair is so blonde, the stylist usually has to bleach in highlights to get a color that will show up. I don't mind, though, since I love that beach-y look.

This guy, however, said I couldn't do highlights, my hair was too blonde, and he wanted to give me lowlights instead. Since I believed my earlier experiences with highlighting had been quite successful, I initially disagreed with him. He insisted, though, and, like I said, I trust a professional hairstylist to know what's best. So I acquiesced, he colored my hair his way, gave it a quick cut and styled it.

Now, I rarely like how someone else styles my hair and I usually make a few adjustments after I leave. Mostly to make it less styled and more casual. But when I saw what he had done, I almost cried. I couldn't fix the fact that I now had brown—yes, brown—poufy soccer mom hair. Not new. Not pretty. Absolutely awful.

A few days later, still trying to make my hair morph into something I could live with or, at least, not cry over, it hit me. The scale of how I look as far as attracting a man is not tipped in my favor. So if I "lose" one of my good attributes, I'm left with even less to offer. And, as we all know, men are visual creatures and you have to appeal to his eyes first before you have a chance to introduce him to your winning personality.

I know I'm clever, interesting, and talented. I've been told I have a sexy voice and a great sense of humor. But does that make any difference if I'm also overweight and aging and trying to hide a bad haircut? Oh, sure, we can repeat our mantra that the right guy will like us just the way we are, but do any of us really believe it?

We definitely *want* to believe it. What a dream-come-true to find someone who thinks you're beautiful, even in sweats, not a stitch of makeup, with a muffin top and paint-peeling bad breath. Fortunately, from what I've seen, once a man is head over heels in love, the object of his affection remains beautiful in his eyes regardless of age, size, or infirmity. Love is blind, I do believe that. But until he's actually in love with you, his vision is twenty-twenty.

That's the way things are, more often than not, and

the sooner a woman accepts it, the better off she'll be. Which means I wear makeup I hope will accentuate my good features, while still being true to myself.

This isn't some anti-feminist rant nor is it the secret to finding a man. (Obviously!) I just think women do themselves a disservice when they don't at least put some effort into appealing to a man's eyesight. Are we really so different? I want a guy who's clean, dresses like he cares, and has a good job. We have superficial expectations for them as they do for us, and it's unrealistic to demand he be everything you want without making any concessions for him.

The good news is looks are subjective. We are all beautiful to someone. It's finding the right someone that's tricky. In the meantime, it behooves us to look our best.

Which is why, after a month of trying unsuccessfully to learn to like my sad, boring hair, I went to a place I trusted and paid another fairly decent bit of cash for a fresh, new cut and platinum blonde highlights. It didn't lead to a man—and that's not why I did it anyway. I felt better about myself, which is vitally important when it comes to being confident. Besides, I've been told, men like that too.

Sigh. I'm such a mess. No, really. Because that's what I think about. Is this attractive to men? Or this? What about that? Short hair? Long hair? A manicure? Should I wear jeans or a skirt? Does this make my butt look big? Actually, that would be a good thing since I'm somewhat lacking in the booty department. But does it make me look thinner? Hotter? Happier? Yes, some colors make me happy. If you feel happy, you're more likely to look happy.

Anyway, I think about these things even when I know there's slim to no chance I'm going to be in the presence of a GWP (Guy With Potential) in the near future. You have to be prepared, right? You could meet someone in the grocery store, at a comedy club, even at your sister's New Year's Eve party. You try so hard to be what the next available guy might want when, deep down, all you really want is someone who wants … you. You, with all your goofy idiosyncrasies and mannerisms, your love of flannel shirts and fuzzy slippers, your off-key singing and tendency to yell at bad drivers. Someone who thinks all your oddities are kinda cute, in fact.

It could happen. I believe! I do! I really do! (What you can't tell is I'm clapping my hands because I also believe in fairies!)

Okay, but I am trying. I was about to say, "*at least* I'm trying" as if I'm getting better at my attempts to believe love is still possible, but that's not true. At one time I found it a lot easier to imagine someone could like me for me. Now I feel a man could only fall for me if I made changes—lost some weight, had a gentler personality, was not writing about being single, and stopped saying what I'm thinking without first thinking about whether I should say it. A kinder, gentler, quieter, thinner Sharyn. But why stop there? Might as well change my name while I'm at it. If I'm going to be someone I'm not, why not call myself Constance or Mercedes or Lady Rowena?

Hey, if I'm going to reinvent myself, I might as well steal my new moniker from classic literature.

Yes, it's a little ridiculous. We've all seen enough Disney movies and *Afterschool Specials* to know how important it is to be yourself. For all I know, I could make those changes and still never meet someone who likes me. Besides, the kind of guy who would like a quieter, gentler Sharyn sounds a bit boring. I would much prefer someone as loud and weird and goofy as I am. Well, maybe not as loud. Unfortunately, it's hard for me to believe a man like that is out there. And if he is, he's either married or not interested.

Which reminds me of *Indiana Jones and the Last Crusade*. That's right. Words of wisdom from an Indiana Jones movie. At the end of the film, Indy's dad is mortally wounded by the villain, Walter Donovan, as an incentive for the younger adventurer to brave death in search of the Holy Grail. Since the Grail purportedly has the power to heal, finding it now appears to be the only hope Jones Sr. has to survive. But two men have already died in the first of three booby traps that await anyone who tries, and Indiana hesitates. Donovan leans toward him and says,

"It's time for you to decide what you believe."

I need to put that on a bumper sticker or a T-shirt; I don't care if it was a movie villain who said it. The line whispers to me at expected and unexpected times.

Sharyn, it's time for you to decide what you believe.

What *do* I believe? Do I believe God loves me and His plan is good and perfect and emanates out of His compassion for me? Or do I believe I'm destined to be alone for the rest of my life?

The point, though, is that I need to *decide* what I believe about God's involvement in my life when it comes to my spinsterness, and I have to do so on a daily basis. If I don't, I may not be prepared for that day when menopause hits … and I turn sixty … and I go for days, months, years without being asked out. The first two will happen—if I live that long—sooner rather than later. The third, well, since I date in short bursts anyway, I'm used to it. But I still need to be prepared for it to continue.

The Bad News

From what I can tell, women long for security. Which means there comes a point when a single woman realizes, "Oh, crap. It's all on me." Instead of working on being a good wife and mother, we have to focus on making sure we have a roof over our heads and food on the table. If we fail, we're out of luck. Unless you have loving, financially capable family members who can bail you out, you're on your own. Which means if you're like me—someone who never cared about having a career and certainly has no interest in management—you *will* struggle.

On the plus side, we live in a time and place that makes independent living as a single woman not the impossible task it once was. In the days of Jane Austen, for instance, unmarried women had few options.

Ang Lee's 1995 version of Austen's *Sense and Sensibility* contains a conversation where Elinor Dashwood says to Edward Ferrars, "You talk of feeling idle and useless. Imagine how that is compounded when one has no hope, no choice of any occupation whatsoever."

Edward, who feels trapped by a controlling mother, replies, "Our circumstances are therefore precisely the same."

"Except that you will inherit your fortune," Elinor concludes. "We cannot even earn ours."

In the movie *Titanic*, which is set in 1912, when Rose complains about how unfair it is that she has to marry a man she doesn't love because they need the money, her mother replies, "Of course it's unfair. We're women. Our choices are never easy."

Though these are cinematic examples, it doesn't take

much research to know we have it better now. Most of the single women I know do just fine—many have high-ranking and/or quality jobs, travel often, and even own their own home. By the time we get to forty, we've pretty much figured out how to enjoy the single life. That doesn't mean it will be easy, but we have a good handle on how it can be done. Still, I have twice come face-to-face with just how fragile personal and financial security can be when the only income you can count on is what *you* bring in.

As I mentioned in chapter one, the first incident took place several years ago when the organization where I worked hit hard times. As a creative writer, my position was an easy one to cut, apparently, so I was laid off. Though I applied for several jobs, nothing happened and, ten months later, I finally gave in to the situation and put my townhouse up for sale. Staying in Colorado no longer seemed an option, so I decided to move to Ohio to be close to family.

Besides losing my income and, within a year, my home, I felt rejected, abandoned, and unwanted. Not only by the company I had given almost a decade of my time, talent, and loyalty to, but by God for putting me in this painful situation.

On the plus side, I was blessed to be able to sell the townhome in five months, despite the housing crisis at the time. That November I packed up my things, said goodbye to the life I loved, and blasted "Brave" by Nichole Nordeman on my car stereo as I started the two-thousand mile trip. After arriving in Ohio, I spent the next six months sleeping on an air mattress in my sister's basement. Through it all, I chose to believe things would only get better.

It didn't work out that way.

First of all, though I had a job interview on my second day in Ohio, they decided to hire someone else. Second, the only other employment possibility at the time was writing for an organization that preached a biblical message I could not agree with. I didn't think it was a good idea but they kept after me for several months and asked me three times to come in for an interview. Yeah, it was nice to be pursued.

Finally, I determined that if God opened the door one more time, I would walk through it. I didn't have much choice. I wasn't making any money but still felt the need to get out of my sister's house and into my own place. It's fine to live with family short-term, but eventually they want to know when they'll get their space back.

With no other option, I felt forced to take the job, which turned out to be a not-so-great experience. So much so that I gained at least twenty pounds in the short time I was there. On the other hand, it was a good learning opportunity, and I had a chance to stand up for what I believe.

Then the company I'd interviewed for when I first moved to Ohio hired me as a freelance writer. When a full-time writing/editing position opened up in that department a few months later, they offered me an interview and, soon after, a job. Naturally, I jumped at the chance. Once again, I was paid to do something I loved. Once again, it was only a matter of time. Because less than three years later, the company hit tough times and, like before, this creative writer was cut.

It was, however, a little better than the first time I got the shaft. I've discovered being laid off is like a divorce. With the Colorado company, I felt like they told me to "get out, we never want to see you again."

But in the second layoff, it was as if they were saying, "We like you and want to be friends, we just can't afford to live with you anymore." In the beginning, anyway. I continued to freelance for them for a few years and maintained relationships with several of the people there.

Still, none of that made up for the fact that, for the second time in my life, I'd been told I wasn't wanted, they no longer needed me, "please box up your stuff, and don't let the door hit you on the way out."

Once more, I found myself navigating the waters of unemployment alone. I suppose I should be used to handling stressful situations without a shoulder to cry on and, in many ways, I am. But you cannot force yourself to be positive and strong all the time. My heart was broken and I felt lost ... again. For several nights that first week, I couldn't stop wondering why I had to go through it twice. It cut like a knife, and my singleness only compounded the fear.

"No man wants me, and I can't keep a job." In the words of Eliza Doolittle, all I could wonder was, "What's to become of me?!"

For the most part, I remained unemployed for almost five years before taking a part-time high school English teacher position in August 2014. It hasn't been easy, but God has been faithful to take care of me, providing freelance work and other opportunities just when I started to worry the money was running out. Best of all, it gave me the time I needed to finish this book.

It's not only in the area of employment where I find my life unstable. Housing can be just as uncertain. I have moved so many times, I couldn't even begin to count the number of places I've lived—not only states (eight to date) but numerous cities within those states, and an untold number of apartments and houses within those cities.

For instance, since I moved to Ohio in 2006, I've lived in seven different towns, taking up residence in one basement, two apartments, one five-bedroom house, a duplex, and, perhaps ironically, a "mother-in-law suite." Most recently, I moved into a little, red house and adopted an abandoned, spunky gray cat I named Neal Diamond because of the diamond-shaped white mark on his throat.

But the big, five-bedroom house a few years ago stands out to me. I had a great roommate and, because it was so spacious, we could host some memorable parties. At the time, I was still working at the marketing job, which provided a suitable income. Things were good.

Nothing lasts forever, though, so when my roommate, Julie, got a housing offer closer to her job, I started thinking about where I wanted to live next. I thought I had plenty of time since our landlords had pleaded with us to stay at least a year, and we had several months until that year was up.

At the same time, the owners were trying to sell "our" house. They had moved to another state, and I could understand their need to unload an unnecessary residence, especially since Julie and I didn't plan to stay. But they sold it sooner than expected and called me one Friday evening to let me know we had three weeks to be out of the house.

Complicating the situation even more, Julie was in Hungary at the time and wouldn't be back for another month and a half. I pleaded with them to let us stay at least until she returned, to no avail. On top of that, I was rehearsing for a musical, which left me with even less time to house hunt.

Now, I know this is really my fault for not signing a lease. But it was too late for that particular regret. So I grudgingly spent the next few weeks trying to find a new apartment, pack, and work, all while singing and dancing for the chorus of *The Music Man* almost every evening and, occasionally, on Saturdays. No pressure, right?

Compounding it all was the massive worry the stress would get to me physically and affect my job. I didn't want to let my boss down, which led me to try even harder to get my work done. On top of all that, I was up until two, sometimes three, in the morning, writing. Thanks, late night muse!

I needed help. I wanted a break. I craved moral support. I found myself envying married women who were going through similar situations but had a partner to walk alongside them. To have someone who could look at apartments while I was at rehearsal or pack the living room so I could get a little extra sleep would have been so nice.

But, as I said, "It's all on me."

If I can't pay a bill, it's all on me. If I have to find another job, I have no other income to count on while I'm looking. If I have to move, who's going to decide where that will be, find the new place, pack the boxes, reserve the truck, change the utilities, figure out where the money will come from, ask people to help—and hope someone will—and have to take care of anything and everything else that might come up? Yeah, that would be me.

As much as I enjoy some aspects of my independence, at times it's just so exhausting. I feel I was meant to have a partner on this journey and I can't believe I'm over fifty and still wandering around trying to handle it alone.

Before you say, "Oh, come on. You're doing fine!" let me add that, when I am employed, I live paycheck to paycheck because I don't know how to handle my finances and I'm terrible about taking care of things like my car or yard or that poor dying Hawaiian Schefflera in my living room. Still, I'm happy to report Neal seems to be doing fine. As far as I can tell.

The good news: I did find a great apartment and moved out just in time. The bad news: I needed a roommate to afford the three-bedroom duplex, which didn't happen, despite months of advertising. This meant I was paying far too much in rent when, as previously mentioned, my company "divorced" me seven months later. This left me unemployed and living in a house I couldn't afford. Not good. Again, I wished I had a partner to help me bear that burden.

But here's the irony, and it's pretty funny when you think about it. Men have told me that one of the reasons I'm single is because I'm too independent.

What the—? Really? What does that even mean? And what other choice do I have? Should I move in with my dad or a sister to prove how vulnerable I am? Of course I'm "independent," but I would think it's rather obvious I'm not very good at it.

I imagine we all know, though, that this is one of those "compliments" men pay single women to make them feel better. Sure, it's preferable to being told "I'm not attracted to you," or "You're boring." But since it means he's not interested, does it really matter why? Hearing I'm "too independent" makes me want to throw something at something ... or someone.

Oh, and by the way, those same men will tell you in the same breath they're looking for a woman with a good career and an income. In other words, we need to need them but not *need* them.

Right.

Feelings

I have a hard time trusting my feelings. They've let me down many times. In my youth, while taking a late-night walk, I saw a young man sitting at a desk in front of a second-story window. For some reason—related, no doubt, to my romance-novelist imagination—my feelings told me I would marry him. I don't know why. As far as I know, I never even met that random boy in the random window.

Another time, my feelings told me I would have two sons and God had great plans for them. These Disney princess emotions had me convinced I would meet the love of my life in Colorado Springs. As you may remember, my second night in town, as I walked to that park for the Fourth of July festivities, I was certain my future husband was in that crowd.

Wrong. Wrong. And so wrong.

As a result, I do not trust my feelings. Even though they're sometimes right. Statistically, they can't always be off. But since there's no way for me to know, I've gotten used to assuming they're wrong and acting accordingly. If my feelings tell me, "This could be it! A perfect time to meet 'him,'" then I am fairly certain it is definitely *not* the time or situation. It's just a crying shame to have such an active imagination that I can see myself meeting someone just about anytime and anywhere. Which means God can't ever surprise me, and I will never fall in love.

How's *that* for logic?

Still, considering the years I've taken up space on this planet, I can safely say there have been numerous ideal situations for love to find me. In my head, I've played out some sublimely romantic scenarios, none of which has yet to come true. As I said, if I imagine it, I can forget about it. I believe they call that a "self-fulfilling prophecy."

If only I could turn my imagination off, but I get caught up in the story and it's hard not to let it play out and see where it goes. This attitude, in many ways, shoots my dream in the foot. I'm trying to get to the place where I can drop my life and future in God's hands and back away.

When I was young—really young, like seven or eight—I believed I could run with superhuman speed. Just three magic words and Zoom!—I was gone. Though I never tested it by racing a car or even my brother, I definitely believed it. Now I'm grown up, and, well, I no longer think I'm a speed racer. But sometimes I have this feeling I might be able to fly.

Every once in a while, I dream about flying, and it's the most natural thing, and I wake up with the thought, "Yeah, I could do that." A part of me believes it's true. I could jump off a building or a mountain and soar through the sky without wings, if I really wanted to.

If I had enough faith.

It's silly. It's crazy. And yet, it's quite possible my belief in being able to fly is, in many ways, stronger than my belief that God could still bring me a husband. Or that He could make my life worthwhile without one. Maybe someday I'll finally be able to see all the beauty in who I am, just as I am.

And I won't only believe.

I will fly.

Story of Hope—S.A.

As a young girl, I assumed I would be married to a loving, committed man with whom I would serve God and others long before I hit fifty. Decades before, actually. I assumed my home would be established, career defined and in place, and I would enjoy the productivity of a healthy, thriving relationship.

Then one day, I woke up. The dreams were a mere vapor. The portrait of my life was being painted but not with the colors, hues, and textures I expected. No marriage, no house, no children. No active, thriving relationship. At all. What went wrong? In a society where couples fit, how should life look without my other half?

Hopeful relationships with young men have presented themselves along this journey and, with each man, expectant hope would reawaken, leading to renewed excitement of potentially joining the forces of the coupled world.

Time and insight, however, would bring accuracy to these moments of hope. This hope led to a false assumption that these men were interested in a committed future with me. With each failed relationship, disappointment and despair would reacquaint themselves as my close companions.

Quieting myself for a moment, faith, time, and hope would again become the foundation on which I would stand. They were and still are necessary for recovery. The process is painful when hope for a certain future is tragically dashed; however, with recovery, hope has always been restored and I continue to grow deeper in wisdom and understanding.

With a clouded view into the future, I decided I would take a chance. I made the decision to embrace life as a single woman because settling for a less-than relationship would only result in a lifetime of minimal fulfillment and maximum frustration.

Working various nine-to-five jobs, I began to pay attention to the spirit of adventure alive within me. I could use all my time and energy trying to find the man of my dreams, or I could do the things I enjoyed. I could be adventuresome, and, perhaps, my prince would find me along the way.

So with an open heart, I determined to embrace the opportunities that crossed my path. And I learned that focusing outside of myself keeps me alive and available to opportunities, experiences, and enjoyment I may have otherwise never been open to before.

With that decision established, my different life began. I took my first adventure to China at the age of thirty-two. I traveled with newly met friends who shared the same love for the international world. Spreading my wings, I visited Switzerland, Austria, France, and England the following year.

For two years in a row, I spent a month in Israel, dancing with an international dance company. This was followed by another trip to China, then Africa and, later, Kazakhstan, before returning to China again, where I am now.

On this journey, I have met new people, made new friends, experienced new lifestyles, eaten mysterious foods, slept in questionable quarters, and walked miles of uncharted territories. My experiences have expanded my world, as I have brought hope to survivors of human trafficking, inhabitants of remote villages, young people with dashed dreams, and comfort to those fleeing war—all experiencing undefined emptiness. With even more opportunities ahead, I look forward to the next adventure.

Although different than my childhood dreams, I have found a way to embrace the good in my world. But with the good has come unexpected adversity. I lost my father and have watched the mental decline of my mother. Then there's the frequent moves, the strained finances, and, sadly, failed relationships.

This is not what I expected at this age but I enjoy the challenges and adventures of living and studying full-time in China.

Do I believe there is man who will join me in the adventures of life and encourage who I am? Yes! Do I take advantage of presented adventures? Yes! Is my life fulfilling and productive? Absolutely! Am I maintaining a heart of gratitude for all I have? Positively!

I daily choose to embrace life—the pleasant, the uncomfortable, the unexpected—and to meet the future, however it may look, believing all of my experiences will mold who I am and who I am becoming.

I never thought I would be fifty years old and unmarried, but I am ... and the journey is good!

S.A.
Student and Adventurer
Shanghai, China

Now, It's Your Turn

- How did you see your future when you were sixteen? Twenty-five? Thirty-nine?

- At what age did you notice the greatest change in your attitude toward your life, if you did? Was it a positive or a negative change?

- What are your biggest challenges as a single woman?

- When do you most wish you had a husband? Why?

- Do you believe a man can love you just the way you are? If not, what would you be willing to change to win his heart? In other words, would you make concessions in order to not be single anymore? Or will you hold out—even forever—for someone who loves you "as is"?

- Work through some of the things you do that "shoot yourself in the foot" as far as relationships go. How do you get in your own way?

Chapter 5

Bargaining
Love the One You're With

And so most women lead lives of quiet resignation, having given up on their hope for a true man.
—John Eldredge, *Wild at Heart*

Throughout my forties, I had a serious memory problem. I kept forgetting my bad experiences with internet dating because the dream and excitement and adventure of possibilities would overwhelm my romantic-minded heart and I'd sign up ... again. Not one to learn from my mistakes, I tend to repeat them, which means I would sign up, laugh or cry my way through a few bad experiences, wonder what on earth I was thinking and let my subscription lapse ... again.

But time would pass, as it always does, and, once again, I would forgot the rudeness and noises and smells and hurts and think, *maybe this time it will work*. Maybe I didn't give it enough time or email all the men I could or say the right things when I did. Maybe I was too—oh, what's that word? Picky. Right. Maybe I was too picky. So I'd sign up and go through the whole sordid experience ... again. Why? Because I could bargain my way into believing just about anything.

The heart is a lonely hunter. And, in my case, one lacking any kind of weapon or ammunition.

Now, the various online dating sites will tell you how important it is to stick with it. *These things take time and you* have to invest in the process if you really want to see results. At least that's what one Eharmony customer service rep told me. Still, devoting a year to the, well, ugliness that is internet matchmaking—and paying for the privilege, to boot—hardly seems like a life-affirming idea.

On the other hand, it has brought wedded bliss to vast numbers of people. If you're willing to take the risk that you might be one of them or accept the consequences if it doesn't work out, why not go for it? This could very well lead you to the man of your dreams! That's what we want, right? *Perhaps this is the time I'll fall in love.*

And we sigh, fill out the questionnaire, and click "yes" when they ask if we're sure we want them to process our payment. All the while praying this time God is guiding us toward our one true love.

As good as it sounded, though, nothing in my series of online dating excursions led me to believe it was the path God wanted me to take toward lifelong love. Oh, the stories I could tell! I wish I could say I've experienced the good, the bad, and the ugly but that would be far too optimistic.

Here are a few standouts:

* *Matt*

I should have ended it as soon as he mentioned he had only been divorced for two months. But, apparently, that particular red flag just wasn't bright enough for me. It was far too easy to be distracted by his flirty intrigues and eager texts. For the first time in more years than I cared to count, someone made me feel desirable, fascinating, even sexy. I lapped it up like a St. Bernard at a swimming hole on a hot, summer day.

To be honest, all this happened before we met in person. In fact, we never met. But it didn't matter. Something happened to my heart in the span of a few days and, for a short time, I was willing to not only ignore red flags, but I refused to even consider the cautions of my own common sense. I had set up my table at the Red Flag Yard Sale and was ready to start bargaining.

We'll call him Matt.

We connected on a Christian dating site where, out of the blue, he requested an instant message conversation. It was the Saturday before New Year's Eve and I was bored and lonely and desperate. This used to happen a lot around the holidays, which was often when I would try internet dating again, year after year. Especially since many sites would have free communication weekends and discounts during that time. (It's like they just *know* when we're most vulnerable!)

Anyway, back to Matt. Before saying yes, I clicked over to his profile so I'd have an idea of who I would be talking to. Imagine my surprise when I saw this comment—in all caps—at the top of his page: "It looks like my ex-wife wants to try to patch things up, so I will not be using this site anymore. Please pray for us, that things will work out according to God's will." Or something along those lines.

Then he asks if I want to chat.

You're right. I should have said no to the message request then and there. But I admit, curiosity got the better of me. I couldn't help but wonder why someone trying to work things out with his ex-wife would IM a stranger on a dating website. So, I accepted the conversation.

Ironically, the first thing Matt wrote was to express his

concern about the fact I was mid-forties and still single. To him, it implied I might be too picky (there's that word again) and hard to please. I countered with my own concerns regarding his recent divorce and potential reconciliation.

Well, it turned out—or so he told me—the ex did not want to reunite; she was just lonely (uh huh) and looking for companionship (right) and he seemed the obvious solution (please). Once he knew what she was thinking, he backed away. Okay. Again, this was what he told me, and I took his comments with a heaping cup of salt.

From the very beginning, though, our conversation clicked. We flirted and teased each other like we'd been dating for months. The more fun I had, the easier it was to forget about that whole recently divorced issue. If he felt ready to move on, who was I to say he wasn't? Besides, it was just so nice to connect with a man for a change.

After about an hour or two of this, Matt asked for my phone number, which I willingly gave him … then he vanished from the conversation. I sent him a few comments. "Hello?" "Are you still there?" Nothing. Uncertain what had happened, I watched a movie while I waited, still hopeful.

He finally called a few hours later and told me he'd lost his internet connection while looking up my town on a map to see how far apart we were. When he discovered it was just a few hours, he was ready to jump in his car and head to Ohio. He wanted to meet me *that night*.

What?! Is this how it feels? Is this it? Yes, I really did go there. But, being the stranger-to-romance girl I am, this freaked me out and I asked him to wait until we got to know each other a little better. He agreed and we continued to chat, by phone, for the rest of the night. Well, a few hours, anyway. Though I tried not to, I found myself recalling all those stories married friends told me about how they just knew he was the one because they talked for hours the first time they met. And it was happening to me! It was magic and poetry and frantically flying red flags all in one delirious phone call.

We talked the next day and the day after that. It was a dream come true. At first. Then it started to get personal. Very personal. I opened up so much that soon he knew I was a virgin who hadn't even been kissed in, well, a long time.

Boy, the things you'll say when you're trying to bargain your way to love. Not even love. Attention. Sweet words. Simply to hear a man's voice in my ear, talking only to me. I got caught up in the moment and said things I never would have admitted to in a more logical frame of mind and certainly not face-to-face. It got so out of hand so quickly that within forty-eight hours the subject of marriage came up. He even mentioned our honeymoon night and promised he would be gentle with me.

As much as I'd enjoyed our conversation up to this point, I have to admit this was an "ew" moment for me. My sister told me it was because a guy I didn't know was already imagining what sex with me would be like. That and the assumption that I want gentle. Guess I'm hoping for something spontaneous and passionate. Gentle sounds far more fragile than I feel about finally being with the man I love. But he didn't know me well enough to know that.

Which was another problem. I'm not sure how much he was actually trying to get to know me as he was trying to *create* me. Not that I can complain; I was doing the same thing with him. We were creating each other in the ideal image of our own wants and desires and loneliness.

I was still willing to take a chance, though, so we tried to figure out when we could meet. At first, we aimed for New Year's Eve. But when Matt had to work late and it became clear he wouldn't arrive until after 8 p.m.—meaning we'd spend the evening and, most likely, the night alone in my apartment—that no longer seemed like such a good idea.

In between phone calls, he sent me texts that said things like "U r so stinkin' cute," and "U wldn't believe the dream I had last night. Wow! I'm even more excited 2 meet u now!" You know, really sweet stuff like that. I wanted it to keep coming. I wanted to tell people I had a boyfriend. This guy actually desired me! Forget all those stupid red flags. Nobody's perfect, right? I had to stop being so dang *picky* and take a chance while I could and just hope we could work everything else out.

We finally decided to meet in Dayton, Ohio, the following Saturday. We'd go to a sports bar for dinner and watch the Steelers in a playoff game. Though he was from Indianapolis and a serious Colts fan, he was willing to watch Pittsburgh play when he found out that was my team. See? How great is that?!

But on Tuesday, New Year's Day, in between his first text and his second, I found out my cousin's twenty-five-year-old daughter had died the night before due to illness. I had lived with this family in-between jobs a decade before and had always been very close to them, so I was devastated by the loss.

Once I could think straight, I sent Matt an email with the tragic news, and told him I would be traveling to Iowa over the weekend for the funeral, meaning we would have to reschedule. I didn't know it then, but that was the beginning of the end.

I didn't hear from Matt for two days after sharing this with him, and, when I did, he expressed his sympathy over the death of my "uncle," and then complained that he hadn't talked to me all week. This was Thursday, by the way, and we'd only known each other since Saturday. His neediness could no longer be ignored and, finally, two weeks later, I sent a long email saying I felt he should take more time to get over his divorce before pursuing another relationship, and, perhaps, he should find someone to mentor him through it.

To be truthful, I know some of this was said out of fear. But I also realized how unwise it would be for me to pursue something with someone who was still in rebound mode. I told him I needed to guard my heart, and I backed away.

A month later—just long enough to make me wonder if I'd made a mistake and to get used to the idea that I'd never hear from him again—he sent me one last email. He told me that, at first, he'd been angry, thinking this never-been-married girl couldn't possibly know anything about relationships. But, after a time, he realized his anger came from the deep-down realization that I wasn't that far off.

To my amazement, he promised to take a break from dating, seek a closer relationship with God, and find counseling. He also said he was canceling his email and dating site accounts. Finally, he added that he planned to hang onto my phone number with the possibility of calling me once he'd worked things through.

As you can imagine, all this impressed me and I found him more attractive than ever. I hoped beyond hope that a few months down the road he'd call.

I never heard from him again. I sincerely hope he was able to get his life together and, since it's been years and I imagine he's been in a relationship for a while by now, I kind of think she might owe me a thank you.

In retrospect, I realize it's possible none of this was true. It felt real, but it's easy to lie online.

For a short time, though, I was more than willing to try to make it happen. I didn't know how long it would be before I had another opportunity like this. And, in fact, he's still my most recent near-miss. Will I be just a little more eager to bargain my way into a relationship the next chance I get?

I'd like to say, "No, I've learned my lesson," but I honestly don't know if that's true.

* Mr. Wonderful

Dear Mr. W~

This will probably come as a bit of a surprise, but I'm afraid I must end our relationship, such as it is. What you may not know is that you are just one in a long line of men I have fallen for, then settled for friendship with in the faint hope that one day your eyes would pop open and you'd see that I was the love of your life.

But your heart is not an option for me. You've given it to someone else and, though she's not interested in it personally, she's locked it in a closet for safe keeping. Or, I should say, to keep it away from other women who might want to love you. You don't seem to mind, despite the obvious pain she is putting you through and, in some pathetic way, I thought I could be the one to help you move on. Silly me.

Instead, I'm the one who's hurting. I can't hear you gush about how wonderful she is anymore. I need to move on.

By the way, you're not going to get this letter and that's okay. I'm doing this for me.

God bless,
~s~

◊◊◊

Have you ever written a letter like that? Or an email? One where you just had to put it down on paper, knowing it would never get into the hands of the person whose name haunted you from the top of the page? I've written such a letter—sometimes it's straight-up poetry—for pretty much every man who's ever broken my heart. Maybe you simply journaled your thoughts. Yeah, I've done that too.

With Mr. W—whom I mentioned in chapter one as a catalyst to my grief and who didn't turn out to be so wonderful for me so perhaps I should call him something else—I needed to face the truth and write it down. I mean, I fell so hard for him, it's been more than a decade and I still have the bruises.

Most of the time, I don't let myself think about him because it hurts too much. Something like that takes time to heal. I needed to write about it. I needed to turn him into a character in a novel and work through the grief vicariously through my main character. Which is exactly what I did. I needed to, eventually, finally, believe myself when I said, "It was for the best."

You see, it doesn't matter that, in the end, he "just wasn't that into me." I was too lost in infatuation to see that. I thought I could change his mind. Did he like me? Maybe. But always between us was his ex-girlfriend, the one he couldn't get over, the one who took him for granted and needed him just enough to not let him go.

If I had thought for a minute it would have made a difference I would have pointed out that loving someone means you want the best for them. He would have said, "You're right," and nodded his head while smiling and gazing into my eyes ... until she called and he rushed to her side because she needed him to install a new dryer vent.

Sadly, I wasted several years of my heart on this guy who would never like me enough. As I write this, besides the internet kerfuffle with the unseen Matt, I have not been interested in anyone since. Sure, there have been a few short-term GWPs, but it didn't take long to recognize the obvious: either he wasn't for me or I wasn't for him. Or both. Usually both. Yet almost every time I can admit I succumbed to a frantic willingness to somehow, someway make it work.

The problem was that I kept making it about him. And this is true about every guy I've had my eye on. Does he like me? Could he like me? Will he like me? But I can't control that. No matter how many times I drove past a guy's house or sent him a sweet note or made him cookies or cake or chocolate cream pie, I couldn't alter his feelings.

Which leads me to the next problem of bargaining: If I can't make the man I'm crazy about fall for me, maybe I can make myself like someone who actually *is* interested. This requires not being so picky.

To Settle Or Not To Settle

I'm saying that the right man for you might be out there right now, and if you don't grab him, someone else will, and you'll have to spend the rest of your life knowing that someone else is married to your husband.

—Marie, *When Harry Met Sally*

Though I tell myself I'm too old and desperate to be picky—having long ago shortened my what-I-want-in-a-guy list to a committed Christian who is, well, breathing—I have to admit it's quite possible I'm more picky now than ever. I've been waiting an eternity, or so it seems. Why settle for anything less than true love? If I don't tell my friends and family, "I'm *so* glad I waited. He was totally worth every year of singleness!" then what's the point?

In *When Harry Met Sally*, Marie and Alice are trying to help Sally move on after a rough break-up, but the conversation takes a bad, if humorous, turn when they face the reality of trying to find the right guy at the right time. Marie warns Sally not to wait, reminding her of a man who died six months after his wife left him.

"What are you saying?" Sally asks. "I should get married to someone right away in case he's about to die?"

Alice replies, "At least you could say you were married."

Sally, played by Meg Ryan, looks at Alice with an expression that is simply priceless—a mix of fear and sadness. I understand that look. I've had similar feelings. Fear that I may never be able to say I was married; sadness that my only option may be to settle for someone I don't adore. And the disappointment of being in this position in the first place.

I've told myself that somewhere out there is a single man who has the qualities I've always dreamed of. Or is it too late to find someone who makes me laugh and has a good job? He doesn't have to be stylish, just clean. A strong and confident disposition would be nice too. Being madly in love with me, of course, is a given.

Okay, slow down, Sharyn. Keep that list nice and short. I need to be realistic. I need to stop being picky and just pick someone. As soon as there's someone to pick. But that's a different topic.

On the Other Hand ...

The more I know of the world, the more I am convinced that I shall never see a man whom I can really love. I require so much!
—Jane Austen, *Sense and Sensibility*

Just as I try to bargain the wrong man into my life, I can also bargain someone out of it by nitpicking every little thing. When I was a senior in high school I dated a guy about ten years older than me. He made me nervous because of his age and how attracted to him I was, but it still didn't take long for me to find that one little thing.

I hate to admit it, but, in this case, we were on our way home from a football game and, other than the soft rock station crooning from the radio, silence filled the car. That's when his nose started whistling every time he breathed out. In that moment, I decided to end it. Was it the only reason? Well, no. I certainly wasn't ready for a relationship with a man in his late twenties. But nose whistling?

In my defense, it turned out to be the right thing to do. Within the next few years this particular fella got two girls pregnant and married one of them. Still, my excuses haven't matured or become more logical. This one's too short, that one's too tall. He doesn't have a good enough sense of humor; he doesn't have the *right* sense of humor. He's too boring. Too young. Too old. Too ... whatever.

As I said, I'm too picky. But that's not the whole story.

A while back I had a writing assignment to interview a woman who had just celebrated her ninety-fifth birthday. When I discovered she had never married, I decided to ask her about it if I had the chance. I had recently started working on *Spinstered* and thought it might be interesting to get the perspective of a woman who was looking back on a single life.

As we sat in her living room, surrounded by years of accumulated knick-knacks and delicate pieces of china, Ruth was relaxed and easy-going and more than willing to answer my questions, even though, at first, she seemed unsure how to express her thoughts on singleness. Because, she told me, she had never talked about it before.

After a moment's hesitation, she said, "Well, I guess I was too picky." But then she added, "I never really felt good enough."

How can a single woman be too picky and have low self-esteem at the same time? It's actually quite easy. We already suspect there's something wrong with us. The idea clings to the perpetually single woman like a frightened cat.

We believe we're not good enough and, at the same time, look down our nose at anyone who might be interested. We get to a point where we can't accept that anyone truly worthwhile would ever want to date us ...

which means if such a person shows up there must be something seriously wrong with him.

And there it is: I'm not good enough for him and he's not good enough for me. Groucho Marx said, "I refuse to join any club that would have me as a member." And, apparently, I won't date someone who would want me as a girlfriend.

It's a stark, unyielding wall of frustration that we keep slamming up against, leaving us feeling more than hopeless. But it all makes sense. Why else would any of us be in this situation? And what do people say? "You need to lower your expectations." Or "Maybe there are areas of your life you need to get in order first."

Even if we don't hear it from outside sources, it still comes to mind. We obsess over our inadequacies, like needing to lose weight or get our finances in order or grow in our relationship with God. At the same time, we stay with someone far longer than we should out of fear of being labeled too picky.

We are pulled in every direction in an attempt to understand our situation and figure out what needs to be done to fix it. It's no wonder that, when I meet a man, I put him on a scale where he either weighs too good for me or not good enough.

Still, it took me years to get to this point. Throughout my twenties and thirties, I fell for many men who made it clear I wasn't what they wanted. Some liked me but not as much as I liked them. I rarely felt pursued.

I did some pursuing myself, with disastrous results, and it's possible I came across as a bit stalker-like, especially in my youth. Following him, driving by his house, calling a radio station and requesting "One on One" by Hall and Oates because he liked basketball.

Dreaming, believing, hoping. Thinking if he only knew how much I liked him, something would happen.

It never worked out that way.

I've moved past all that now and, I suppose, have a little more self-respect. But that doesn't mean I won't still overdo it. I was, am, and will always be a hopeless, hopeful romantic who can't relax and let God handle it. You might not be quite as date-free as I've been, but don't we all know what it's like to hope? And then do all those silly things to get his attention: talk too loud, flip our hair, touch his arm, giggle at every ridiculous thing he says. Or we wear too much makeup, show too much skin, all while trying *not* to seem desperate. Sheesh.

It's so easy to latch on to optimism, only to find ourselves going completely overboard. And, in doing so, we drown our dreams in our misguided attempts to be what we think he's looking for.

My friend, Lisa Anderson, director of Boundless.org and author of *The Dating Manifesto: A Drama-Free Plan for Pursuing Marriage with Purpose* (releasing August 2015), wrote this in an article titled "Finding a Great Husband Doesn't Just 'Happen'" for *Today's Christian Woman*:

> *Women are notorious for giving up too much for very little in return. In relationships, it's usually time, attention, emotional connection, affection, and sex. We give it all with no expectation of commitment or even exclusivity. For me, I gave guys access to my time and emotions far too early on in a relationship. I was always available, always willing to talk, and always an open book. Where was the mystery? More telling, where was the motivation to pursue me when I was already throwing myself at their feet?*

We just want them to notice and, when they do, it's so easy to get caught up in making it work, come what may. Even that single guy you met at the office party, the one you know is completely wrong for you, can meet your minimum qualifications—male, the right age, and a decent job—to make you willing to go out a second time. Then a third and a fourth and who knows how many dates you can bargain yourself into because he's there and he's interested and, please God, you want to move forward *into* something for a change. Even if it's the wrong something.

Though past experiences say I'm far more likely to end things too early, I have watched many a girl hang onto a relationship long past its expiration date, hoping it will, magically, become what she wants. I understand that. No one wants to let go of a good thing, fearful she'll make the mistake of missing out on a great catch because she was too hard to please. It's the same concept as not wanting to pursue a man too aggressively because you don't want to come across as desperate.

But why shouldn't we be a bit choosy when it comes to the person we want to spend the rest of our lives with? How many times has someone told you, "It's better to be single than to be stuck in a bad marriage"? And let's not forget "the heart wants what the heart wants."

To clarify, I don't like the "heart" saying when used as an excuse for sin, but there is truth in it. We all have our ideal—and heaven only knows what that has become after years of romantic comedies and sweet daydreams. Is it so wrong to want that first kiss to lift you off the floor, a few butterflies when he walks into the room, a certain something in his eye he saves just for you? Or is it enough to know he's a good man who serves the Lord and will love and care for you and, if you have any, your children?

But who am I kidding? We want it all. We've been saving up our love and passion for years, decades even, and we're ready for all of those dreams to come true.

Okay, so, we're hard to please. But are we too unbending in our requirements? If we're dismissing a perfectly lovely man because he likes hip hop, has no sense of style or, ahem, whistles through his nose, it may be difficult to find someone perfect enough to meet such ideals ... ever. The older I get the more I re-think my preferences on looks, even chemistry. Besides, I fully believe attraction can grow over time.

Still, we also need to get to a place where we believe we're worthy of something beautiful. If the God of the universe delights in us, His children, why can't a man? A simple, normal, godly man who truly loves me just the way I am.

That's a bargain worth waiting for.

---

* *Not the person's real name.*

Story of Hope—Carla

My story of hope has certainly had its share of peaks and valleys. Relationships with men have ranged from unrequited love to feeling overwhelmingly smothered. I tend not to give up easily on a relationship and I try to make it work well past the expiration date.

An unhealthy relationship a few years ago taught me that I needed to stop the cycle of believing I have to be married to be content. As I came out of that relationship, I decided I needed to reassess what was good, what was so-so, and what was unacceptable about it, and then determine how I would do things differently next time. I went to the one source that has grounded me: God's Word.

Ephesians 5 showed me what the Lord wanted from me as a wife. I meditated over Titus 2, learning what He wanted from me as a woman who is maturing in life and in my relationship with Him. I studied the character traits of a pastor in 1 Timothy 3, knowing these would be great qualities for a husband. I also remembered how the Lord calls us to seek counsel from other believers, so I employed that truth by surrounding myself with godly women who would tell me what I needed to hear. And I prayed ... a lot.

What I gained from this reflective time served me well when Mark came into my life. We had known each other for several years by being in the same business circles, and I had always enjoyed his sense of humor.

Mark is a man with a consistent smile on his face and eyes that dance. He is one of the most grace-filled men I've ever met. Above all, he loves the Lord and boldly lives his faith. He seemed to appreciate my desire to walk closely with Christ and wasn't intimidated by my strong personality. During the first few dates, it became clear to me that we had some differing convictions, and I knew if I were to be the kind of wife I desired to be, these could be potential deal-breakers.

The talk of marriage started early in the dating process as we discussed what we expected from a potential spouse, how we fit each other's desire, and how ministry would look for us as a couple. It was a whirlwind romance with the "I love you" conversation happening much quicker than I'd ever imagined it would. I know the speed with which we moved and the temptation of finally being married had greatly enticed me to ignore the lessons learned.

But God never let me go. The Lord calls a woman to respect her husband and follow him. This was where the deal-breaker occurred for me. While Mark and I had Jesus in common, we weren't spiritually heading in the same direction. Issues of doctrinal difference put me in a position where I couldn't follow him as God's Word called me to do.

Ending the relationship with Mark was messy and difficult. It was so hard for me to explain the why because we weren't technically wrong in being together. We were equally yoked by the most basic definition of that phrase. Yet equal yoking means so much more than just being believers in Jesus Christ. It means we are moving in the same direction. Mark and I would have been dragging each other along in the hope of changing the other's mind/conviction.

Still, my heart wanted him. He thought I was beautiful and smart. He wanted me. He wanted us to marry and spend the rest of our lives together. That is some powerful emotion to try to battle. The temptation to throw caution to the wind and do what I wanted to do was intense. Those emotions led me to make decisions that caused more heartache because I found it so difficult to let go. I tried to bargain or manipulate the truth to make it work. Because of that, the break-up wasn't as clean as it needed to be. At times, I couldn't concentrate or think clearly. I continued to search out the Word to help me figure out what to do.

I found the Lord wants me to have a sober mind so I can be discerning about life-altering decisions. That sobriety comes from saturating my mind with Scripture. One passage that helped me greatly was 1 Peter 1:13–14.

While I haven't done everything "perfect," because of His mercy, I came out of it with much less heartbreak than previous times. He has abundantly blessed me with the peace of knowing He has an awesome plan for me and my life—with or without a husband.

Carla Ewing
Director, Women's Ministry at Maple City Baptist Church
Monmouth, IL

Now, It's Your Turn

- Have you ever stayed in a relationship too long? Why? What did you learn from the experience?

- What are some things you feel you need to change about yourself before someone could love you? How do you feel about that?

- Do you think you could turn down a potential relationship if you felt it wasn't right or possibly even against God's will? Would your friends and/or family members speak up if they thought saying something was necessary? Would you listen? How do you feel about these questions?

- Has anyone ever accused you of being too picky? What were their reasons? Were they right or wrong? Why or why not?

- What do you think is beautiful and unique about you? What have others told you? Find a few really good friends and ask them.

98

Chapter 6

Guilt
Lonely Is the Night

... if two lie down together, they will keep warm;
But how can one be warm alone?
—Ecclesiastes 4:11

I like men. God help me, I do. I like the way they talk and think. I like the way they laugh at dumb Jim Carrey movies and yell at football refs. I like their strong hands, big egos, and one-track minds. And if they smell like cold air and leather and a hint of cologne, it does crazy things to me. Knees: weak. Head: swooning. Imagination: soaring. Dreams: priceless.

Of course, all this weakening, swooning craziness can lead to inappropriate, confusing, what-am-I-gonna-do-with-them thoughts. Sometimes I can't *not* look at men. In moments, when a man I like stands so close I can feel him breathe, I pause and sigh and wish he would move even closer. My mind takes me into the embrace of a relationship and I falter there, letting myself feel the dream until I can hardly bear it.

Things have improved with time. The tears fall less often now, but I can still feel like I'm turning in circles, wanting something that always seems out of reach. I know I can take the longing, lay it at Jesus's feet, and back away, but that's easier said than done. Instead, I tend to cling to it. *This is a perfectly natural desire, Lord. I shouldn't have to give it up.* So often, though, He remains silent and, in low moments under harsh lights, I wonder if God just doesn't care.

Why do I do this to myself? I know I shouldn't go there—wanting something that's not, at the moment anyway, possible. But the dream of it is such a sweet space and the brief, false joy I find seems to make the guilt I feel later almost worth it.

Almost.

The Waiting

I don't know about you, but when I made the decision to wait for sex until marriage, I had a slightly shorter timetable in mind. One where I actually had sex while still energetic enough to enjoy it. Not that I would have done things any differently if I had known I would one day find myself waving goodbye to fifty and still waiting.

The whole virginity thing—which seemed so romantic and sweet and special when I was twenty—started to feel a bit lonely and pathetic and, even worse, to reek of repression about five years ago. Which isn't me. As much as I can tell, I'm a passionate woman who can't wait to enjoy all that good stuff with the right man. In the meantime, though, what's a girl to do with all of these pent-up feelings?

Seriously. That's not a rhetorical question. What do I do? Well, we'll get to that. But first, a funny sex story. Actually, it's a funny story about *not* having sex. Because that's my life ... at the moment anyway.

A few years ago, I attended the last segment in a four-part singles seminar titled "Holy Sex." The speaker focused on alternatives. Alternatives to sex, to be specific. *Now we'll get some answers!* I suppose I had certain expectations, coming from my particular perspective, but imagine my surprise when the speaker—who was married, of course, because married people know so much about the single life—suggested taking up a hobby. Like knitting. Yes, he actually suggested two needles and a big ball of yarn will heal what ails all of us burning, yearning singles.

Only someone who's getting some on a regular basis would think knitting or reading or badminton would suffice as any kind of substitute for sex, let alone a satisfying one.

It's not that I wanted him to talk about masturbation in this room full of mixed singles, but I expected him to at least touch on the subject. No pun intended. Okay, yes, that was on purpose. I mean, the whole thing was pretty laughable. Knitting. Good grief. I wonder how he would have felt if he had strolled into his bedroom that night, thanking God for the gift of marriage, only to have his wife stick a hand in his face and say, "Not tonight, dear. I'm knitting you a sweater."

We know it's not an easy or comfortable subject. Back in the 1990s, *Seinfeld* famously made fun of it when the friends set a wager to see who could remain "master of his domain" the longest. Just a little reminder that many do it but few talk about it. And we don't need to talk about it. The issue isn't whether or not it's an alternative, the issue isn't what we say or don't say, it's the thought-life behind what we do. When those lustful thoughts come, do I dwell on them ... or do I pursue purity?

To be honest, I've gone through phases. I could slide along for months without caving, then, usually without warning, the longing would hit me just right and I'd make the decision to watch something I shouldn't watch or listen to something I shouldn't hear or take a simple daydream and let it go further than it should. Some days are easier than others.

Much like every other sin I deal with.

And the sin is quickly followed by guilt. "Great. I failed again. Back to square one." I'm disappointed in myself. God must be disappointed. I want to make purer choices with my heart and mind; I want to please Him by pursuing a life of purity. Yet I continually fail.

If I'm going to continue on in this vein of honesty, I have to now admit that I have occasionally tried to avoid my feelings of guilt by pointing out a few things to God. Because, you know, He might be too busy to notice.

For instance, at times I've felt I needed to remind Him that if I were married I would have a sexual outlet. Because, in my tunnel-vision naiveté, I believed sex within the confines of a committed, loving marriage would solve my problems. Well, at least one of them, anyway.

"Yes, you would have an outlet," He'd respond, "but you would still struggle with temptation. It would just be different."

Clearly, He didn't understand, so I said, "Not necessarily. Why would You think that? Without my sexual frustration as a distraction, maybe I could concentrate on other things."

"All I'm asking you to do, Sharyn, is face the truth of your weaknesses and deal with them now. No more excuses. No more pity parties or pointing fingers. Just raw honesty between you and Me."

I held back a laugh. "Easier said than done."

"Well, then," He said, and it's possible He actually did laugh, "it's a good thing I've given you all the strength and wisdom you need to resist temptation."

In other words, when I choose sin, I alone am to blame.

Still, I'm hardly the first person to try to turn the focus off myself when it comes to sin. If I could convince God—and myself—it's not my fault and I did everything in my power to resist, maybe I could sleep a little better. But I can't so I don't. Our society doesn't help, wanting to excuse sin by offering us an out. This explains the popularity of tolerance. If I give your sin a mark of approval, then you can't condemn mine. We think we can all get away with something. And we end up with a society that shuts its eyes to sin.

It's so much easier to put all my guilt and frustration on God's hefty shoulders.

"I want to remind You," I've often said, "that You actually have the power to change my situation. If You just brought me a husband, for heaven's sake, I wouldn't have this problem. Yet here I sit, gripping the arm rests with sweaty hands. It's too hard. Can't You give me an out?"

"Of course I could. But I won't." Then He'd add, "I realize it's hard. All temptation is. Stop looking for loopholes and prove your love for me through unquestioning obedience."

Okay, now I'm oh-for-two. And I admit to feeling a tad frustrated when I don't get the answers I want.

"I don't think it's particularly fair, Lord, that You've put me in this position."

And He replied, "When did I ever promise you fair?"

Touché.

He continued, "Need I remind you, Sharyn, of all those who suffer because of disease or who have recently lost a loved one or who struggle just to get through each day, whether physically, financially, or emotionally? You have a loving family, good friends, your health. How can you complain about this one hole in your life?"

Turns out, it's pretty easy to do.

Hello, guilt.

More Finger-pointing

Tom Petty once sang about how good girls sit at home with broken hearts. Too bad we end up blaming ourselves for that. But let's get back to men, shall we? It's not *all* their fault, but I do believe they are somewhat to blame for the overabundance of single women, standing dazed and confused in their kitchens on Friday nights, trying to decide between Stouffers lasagna and Bob Evans take-out. That's not you, of course, but there are a few of us out there.

Anyway, we're talking about men here.

As I mentioned earlier, I love 'em. I really do. But they're not stepping up. For whatever reason—and I have my theories—men, Christian ones specifically, seem to have fallen into the realm of passivity. I'm not just speculating here. This conclusion is based on years of observation and numerous conversations. Marriage means maturity, and, it would seem, some men just aren't interested in either.

Boundless, a Focus on the Family webzine for Christian singles and young adults, first introduced me to a term for this: adultescence—an extended adolescence that covers the ages of eighteen to twenty-nine ... and beyond. Yes, I personally know a few adultescents in their forties and fifties.

The word has, in fact, been around since at least 2004.

In December of that year, *The New York Times* published an article titled "2004: In a Word; Adultescent." The writer, John Tierney, stated, "Since 1970, the median age for Americans to marry has risen four years, to twenty-five for women and twenty-seven for men. Meanwhile, the proportion of people in their early thirties who have never married has tripled."

That was over a decade ago. In March of 2013, the average age for a first marriage had continued to rise to twenty-seven for women and twenty-nine for men.

In my day, a man with no interest in stepping up to the marriage altar was called—or chose to be called—"a bachelor 'til the Rapture." And most of them said it with pride. Like it was this club that met in a neighborhood tree house and you had to climb a knotted rope to get to it. And of course only the cool kids could join.

So, not only do we see evidence all around us of lazy, unmotivated boy-men, but I've personally encountered some. A few of my single, male friends have told me they won't ask a woman out, preferring to wait for her to take the first step. Why? They say it's because they don't want to get hurt. That might be true. But they also have decided they deserve to be the pursued instead of being the pursuer, turning God's design on its head. Bald, chubby, forty-something guys clinging to the idea that some hot, young thing will find them irresistible. In other words, they want to be treated like the woman. Wow, we find that *so* attractive!

One conversation led me to tell an acquaintance of mine that he would be wise to consider how important it is for a woman to feel safe and secure in a relationship. If he wasn't willing to take a risk in the relationship from the very beginning but, instead, chose to guard his own ego, how could she ever trust him to protect her?

He responded, "Well, I want to feel safe too."

Ugh. I choose to believe he is an extreme exception.

When it comes to this role reversal, I lay the majority of the blame at the feet of a group of people who, in my opinion, have done more harm to women than we can imagine. And they've done it all in the name of women's rights. Yep, I'm talking about feminists. In their self-centered push to grab more power for women, they've managed to strip both sexes of their unique, individual strengths. The result? A lot of unhappy and unsatisfied females.

The desire for marriage and children, whether feminists like it or not, is universal. I see it come up in movies and on TV shows all the time.

Take, for instance, the sitcom *Friends*. One episode was about what the characters went through as they each turned thirty. At Rachel's birthday party, she received a card from Chandler and Monica that read:

Happy birthday, Grandma!
It's better to be over the hill than buried under it.

With tears flooding her eyes, Rachel laughed and told them it was funny, though she clearly didn't feel that way. Chandler rushed to her side. "That was a joke!"

"No, I know. I get it," Rachel said, obviously trying to keep the tears from taking over. "It's funny."

Still trying to right a wrong, Chandler put a hand on her arm. "Because you're not a grandmother."

Rachel replied, "No, I know. Because to be a grandmother you have to be married and have children and I don't have any of those things."

Then she ran out of the room, sobbing.

Of course, characters like Rachel, the show regularly

made clear, weren't held back by any no-sex-before-marriage restriction. Most if not all of her relationships ended up in the bedroom, usually fairly quickly. Feminism would tell us that should make her feel happy and fulfilled. But even the writers knew that wasn't true.

Because we simply cannot change how God made us. For most of us, that's the desire to love our husbands and nurture our children and build a home and develop meaningful relationships.

But instead of waiting for meaningful, we settle for "sexting" and one night stands.

No wonder we're lonely ... and alone.

Shut Up

This loneliness has led—or at least contributed—to a change in my heart over the last few years, and it's disconcerting. It's a thought that tickles my conscious, telling me things have altered and not in a good way. Around the time I turned forty, my until-then vibrant hope for marriage took a serious nosedive. One day, I realized I could not imagine a circumstance in which I could meet someone I might fall in love with. It no longer seemed possible and my daydreams, once alive and achievable, appeared distant, even ridiculous.

Taking these feelings into consideration made the commitment to save sex for marriage even more difficult. I'm not saying I wouldn't, but my mind seemed a little less settled on the idea. What was a charming and romantic conviction in my twenties became a mantra of loneliness in my thirties. Then, as I hurtled through the next decade toward my fiftieth birthday, the "true love waits" promise stopped being an isn't-that-sweet? dream and started feeling more, in a word, sad. Even today, I sometimes think it sounds like nothing more than a desperate attempt to believe I will be in a loving, committed, intimate relationship someday. And that I have the patience to wait for sex until then.

So, again, I find myself looking for loopholes. I wouldn't be the first virgin who decided to hold out until a certain age and, once that age was reached, all bets—or promises, as the case may be—were off. Something along the lines of, "If I'm not married by the time I'm fifty, I'm going to find someone to sleep with. I do *not* want to die a virgin!"

Sex is a perfectly natural desire. A girl should be able to do something about it eventually. Sure, there are risks involved, but, for heaven's sake, I'm a repressed single woman whose best years seem to be behind her. Wouldn't a night of passion be an exciting change of pace? Not that I would go out looking for it. I just worry I might not be too quick to dismiss the idea if an opportunity were to present itself. Besides, shouldn't there be a statute of limitation, as it were, on that chastity promise I made back before I had wrinkles and age spots?

Oh, who am I kidding? I'm not going to run out and sleep with some guy. Feeling repressed and frustrated doesn't change the fact the Bible says sex outside of marriage is sin. And it doesn't change how strongly I feel about being obedient to God in this. Whether I like it or not.

That said, I did come close to giving in several years ago. A new co-worker, who reminded me of *The Mummy* actor Brendan Fraser, had been flirting shamelessly with me at the office. Though I didn't like the awkwardness of the situation, I lapped up the attention. When he asked me to meet him late one night I was ready. For anything. Swamped in loneliness, I couldn't talk myself out of it. At least, for a night, I would feel something, experience something more than another evening of watching *Scarecrow and Mrs. King* reruns while swallowing Snickers bars whole and guzzling diet Coke.

Looking back I know this decision was a gesture—and not a very nice one—to God. "You want me to be single? Fine. But You can't stop me from having sex."

Be careful about telling God what He can or can't do. Turns out, He could stop me. And He did. As I stared at my keys, working up the nerve to walk out the door, my phone rang. A friend I hadn't talked to in about a year called me out of the blue because she had a feeling she should. Without much prodding, I spilled. Everything. What I'd been going through and what I was about to do.

And this calm, wise voice said, "Sharyn, don't be stupid. I know you're lonely, but don't do something you'll regret."

We talked for about an hour and by the time I hung up, the moment had passed. I didn't have any trouble resisting "Brendan" after that. When I found out later he had recently separated from his wife, I realized just how much heartache God had saved me from.

But guarding my heart is just one of several reasons to resist this temptation. Top of the list is the promise I made to God oh so many years ago. This wasn't some airy pledge whispered into the atmosphere by a clueless, dream-walking teen but a purposeful vow to Him when I was old enough to know exactly what I was doing. Even if I hadn't made that promise, I still have to go back to what the Bible says: Sex outside of marriage is sin. (Hebrews

13:4, for one example.) But though I wish I could say my commitment to chastity was purely based on my love for God, my long list of sins proves that's not true.

No, I would say there are two main reasons I'm still a virgin: One is because of God's love for me—like the aforementioned phone call, He's kept me from taking that step. And the other is my love of romance and the belief that I've been waiting for something amazing. I have long wanted my story to be one for the ages. The kind people want to write about. The kind *I* want to write about. Which means I spend a lot of time dreaming about something unrealistic and then, if someone flawed and normal shows up, it becomes too real and I scurry into a corner.

In other words, I'm afraid I'll never have sex and spend my life frustrated … and I'm afraid I will and, instead of satisfied, I'll be disappointed.

There's a scene near the end of the movie *The 40-Year-Old Virgin*—you knew I'd have to mention it at some point, right?—where the main character, Andy, tells Trish, the women he's fallen for, that he hadn't tried to have sex with her because he was a virgin, and he was afraid it wouldn't be good. Trish responds that of course it will be good because they're in love.

Ah, the magic of movies. (A caveat: I can't recommend this movie because of the language and sexual content. It definitely earns its R rating. I'd recommend a cleaned-up version but there might not be much of a movie left.)

Sex isn't the answer anyway. My body likes to distract me and make me think physical intimacy will do more for me than meet a need. It doesn't help that I suspect, worry, wonder if it wouldn't be too hard for someone to seduce me if he were to put his mind to it. But no one has—not really—and I tell myself that's a good thing. Though somewhat embarrassing and a blast to my self-esteem, it's good because I haven't found myself in a situation that could lead to sexual sin. Bad because it seems like less than a handful of men have found me attractive enough to even attempt something.

Being the optimist I am, though, I've sought ways to feel better about the whole thing. This took me back to the belief that these events were all God's way of protecting His child. It's all done out of love! How could I not be thankful for His watch-care over me? I was ... and am. Of course, I am. But within that acceptance lurked the feeling that I just wasn't appealing. No one wanted me—not enough, not for a night, and certainly not for a lifetime.

In this respect, I can understand any woman who hasn't waited. My life experience has been different but it could have just as easily gone another way. Whether you are in a physical relationship now or have recommitted yourself to purity, you have similar struggles to mine. Our needs—that ache we share to be held close and loved—are the same.

Besides, I haven't been perfect. Yes, I'm a virgin. But the older I get the less admirable that is. At least, to me. Plus, I sometimes feel cheated and wonder why I've tried so hard to do what I thought was right, when, perhaps, I would have been happier putting God's will on the back burner until I needed Him again. He would forgive me if I asked Him. Aren't some of the most awe-inspiring and beautiful stories those of redemption after great sin? Who wants to watch a movie or read a book about someone who never messes up but goes through life being good? Or, at least, not doing anything *that* bad.

Like me. Though I can't say I lived the pure and holy

life God called me to, I never fell into a deep pit of sin where I turned my back on Him completely. There was, however, a time when I felt abandoned by God. My mom had died, I had no career direction, and I didn't have a boyfriend.

So I rebelled. Nothing too aggressive, just the mild revolt of a twenty-something good girl who wanted to walk on the other side of the right-and-wrong line for a while. This included swearing, taking a few puffs on a cigarette, and, occasionally, going out to bars with friends. Basically, the kinds of things most people do in high school. As for men, I did make out with a stranger in the back seat of a car once. ...

Okay, I'll just tell you what happened. It was a Friday night and my friend, Shelley, and I decided to enjoy a night on the town. We went to a bar near West Point, NY, and I was feeling a bit dangerous. It was ladies' night, which meant drinks were cheap. Since I was also fairly new to alcohol, I wasn't sure what to order, so I tried several different concoctions. It probably won't surprise you to hear I got a little tipsy. Scratch that. I was fall-on-the-floor drunk.

In my inebriated state, I made the brilliant decision to flirt with one of the bouncers. The next thing I knew, my friend was in the front seat with the guy she'd stumbled into while I was in the back being groped and slobbered on by a Mr. Clean lookalike who tasted like dirty socks.

And what did I do? I fell asleep. He was kissing me and touching me in a way no man had before, and I was out like my satellite service during a storm. Which, by the way, was how I found out drinking isn't any fun because it makes me sleepy.

I did wake up a few times and thought, "He's still

kissing me. Why is he still kissing me?" But I didn't try to stop him, despite the fact I didn't enjoy it. I guess, in a way, it seemed like it was about time; I might as well get it over with.

Still, by the grace of God, my friend and I held off the guys from taking it further than making out in a car. At one point, we drove to a restaurant to use the bathroom. While my friend took care of business, I sat on the floor. And we sobbed like we'd just seen our dog get hit by a car.

"I'm just not ready," I said. "Why doesn't he understand that?"

Yes, I actually thought he cared how I felt. Drunk and naïve. It's a pretty pathetic combination.

Somehow, though, we finally convinced them to take us to my friend's house, which was where I had left my car. I let him kiss me for a bit longer, then something inside me said, "Get out now!"

I crawled over him instead of going out my door—I don't know why—pulled the handle and half-fell out onto the pavement, ran to my car and drove home, sobbing all the way. I felt dirty and gross and all stirred up and ready for more.

Yes, I could have lost my virginity that night and it wouldn't have been that unusual a story. Still, it would have had a serious, negative impact on my life. In this case, God saved me from my own stupidity.

Can I say I've lived a godly, pure life? No. But that night was my lesson—on drinking, on men, on my own inability to show restraint. I learned a lot about myself.

And I haven't been kissed since. This may be one of the saddest truths of my spinster life. One regrettable, disappointing make-out session over a quarter of a century ago might be the best I ever get in the kissing department.

I sure hope not, but it might. Why? What could I have done to make myself so un-kissable?

I don't know. What I do know is that I chose to make a vow to God years ago and now must accept the fact that I might never have sex, let alone experience any kind of intimacy with a man again.

This is my human history, based on my decision to follow God along with the good and bad choices I've made. I don't want to sin, but I do want to be desired. I want to be a woman in the arms of a man, aware of my skin and my heart and what it feels like to be that close to someone. God, in His mercy, understands my weakness and has stood between me and a big mistake.

Whether I wanted Him to or not.

The Way of All Flesh

I don't know how I feel about my breasts. They haven't been much use to me, other than as a bra-filler. They certainly haven't fulfilled their main purposes—to nourish children and to please my husband. No, my boobs just sit there in all their double-D glory, getting in my way and causing more than their fair share of embarrassing moments. For the most part, though, I stuff them in a brassiere, hide my cleavage behind sensible shirts, and, because I've been warned based on my family history, check regularly for lumps.

Still, sometimes I think, *that can't be what God intended, can it?* He created breasts, molding woman into something softer than man, giving us those extra curves, like beacons of femininity. King Solomon was certainly fond of them; the bridegroom mentions his lover's breasts eight times in

Song of Solomon.

It's Proverbs 5:19 that most stands out to me, though, when Solomon encourages his sons to love their wives: "A loving doe, a graceful deer—may her breasts satisfy you always, may you ever be intoxicated with her love" (NIV).

"Intoxicated with her love." Wow. Can you imagine? I can but try not to. Why upset myself unnecessarily?

Merriam-Webster has three definitions for "breast": the two soft parts on a woman's chest that produce milk, the front of someone's body, and the place where emotions are felt. It's the latter that resonates with me. Put your hand over your heart. This is where our feelings live. Our hurts, our disappointments, our fears, and, yes, our desires. It's all connected. God made it that way.

Maybe if I can stop seeing certain body parts as useless because of my sex-free life, I might be able to start enjoying me as a whole more thoroughly. I am not separate from my body. So why do I keep seeing myself that way?

Virgin Daughter

Are you familiar with the story of Jephthah and his daughter? Well, if you aren't, I recommend you go to Judges 11 and read it carefully. And if you do know it, maybe read the account again? In fact, if you would do so right now, then come back, that would be dandy.

I'll just wait here.

Give you a few minutes.

Until you're done.

Okay?

Sad story, huh? I know there's some discussion over whether or not Jephthah actually sacrificed his daughter as a burnt offering. Not wanting to get into a deep theological discourse on the topic, I personally don't think that's what happened. My Ryrie Study Bible (NASB) states the verse containing Jephthah's vow could be translated: " ... shall surely be the Lord's (if a human being comes first), *or* I will offer it up for a burnt offering (if an animal appears first)."

I find it highly unlikely that God would bless someone for vowing to sacrifice a person—particularly a child—as a burnt offering, especially considering child sacrifice was a Canaanite practice He clearly found detestable (see Lev. 18:21, 20:2–5; Jer. 32:35). It seems completely out of character for God to allow this to happen in His name, then list Jephthah as a hero of the faith in Hebrews 11.

Still, it's a strange vow. Clearly, he expected something living to come out "of the doors of my house to meet me when I return ..." Was he assuming it would be his dog—or whatever kind of pet they had back then? I can't believe he thought a sacrificial sheep or cow would exit the house first. Perhaps he and his wife weren't getting along and he saw this as an easy out. (I kid, of course. Because that would be wrong.) But he must not have considered the possibility that his daughter would lead the celebration of his victory at battle.

Regardless of what was going through his head, Jephthah's hasty vow had a long-lasting effect. Not only did it end his daughter's hope for marriage and children, but it ended his genealogical line since she was his only offspring.

But here's what stood out for me: She didn't weep for her life or her future, she wept for her virginity and consequential childlessness. To be more specific, she asked her father for two months to wander the hill country, "bewailing" her forced chastity with her friends. Then she returned home, ready to accept her fate, and, Scripture says, "She knew no man." (Again implying she never married, not that she was killed.) This was such a terrible fate that, from then on, Israelite women spent four days a year lamenting Jephthah's sad, virgin daughter.

I can relate. My single friends and I have mourned our own sexless lives while hiking through the mountains of Colorado, inhaling ice cream at an Ohio dairy, and zipping through the ocean waves of the Dominican Republic on a catamaran. Grief has followed me everywhere. I've wept for my virginity. It's not something I've held up as a badge of honor and purity, but something I hid, worried it only served as a sign of my childless undesirability.

What if I am unlovable? Yes, it's a terrible question and if I said this to my friends they would cluck their tongues and shake their heads and wonder how I could even ask such a thing. I wish it weren't so easy to believe, but I started to question my unlovability after only a few years of rejection. When you see sillier, chubbier, stranger women tying the knot, the question "What's wrong with me?" seems like a natural response.

This has been a tough part of the grieving process for me. I've had to work through my negative attitude, deal with my guilt over wanting sex, and find a way to think positively about the whole thing. It would be nice if I could reach a level of peace before my guy comes along. On the other hand, getting married would solve some of these issues. Wouldn't it?

Now, I realize it's not actually sex I'm weeping over. Sure, that's part of it, but, to be honest, what I really long for is intimacy. More than just the physical stuff, I want emotional intimacy. Hang on here with me because I'm about to go into serious romance novelist mode. Because that's what I am, at heart. Consider yourself warned.

Have you ever seen a couple in love? Of course you have. So have I. And usually what lets you know they're in love isn't so much what they say but what they don't *have* to say. The looks that let you know something just passed between these two people that we can't know. It's theirs alone. A smile, a nudge. A sigh. At times it's almost electric.

A few years ago, while working in the marketing department at a liberal arts university, I was walking across campus with several co-workers and our student intern. We knew this intern was in a serious relationship, but I hadn't yet met her boyfriend. As we made our way toward the student center, I saw a young man coming toward us, driving a golf cart, which some employees do when their work takes them regularly from building to building. When he passed us, this boy and our intern exchanged a look that could be felt. Neither said a word.

Glancing at the beaming young girl, I asked, "Was that him?" She nodded. I added, "Well, I certainly hope so. Because if he's not, he should be. I almost felt the electricity between you two."

What they had was obvious to everyone who saw it and, to a degree, almost supernatural. They're married now.

Another time, I was hanging out with a few friends, including a recently engaged couple. The girl said something funny, and her fiancé smiled at her. That's it. He simply smiled. But a woman who witnessed the exchange said, "Wow, you are so in love with her." We all laughed because it was that evident. Yes, now they're married too.

That's what I want. A connection you can't explain.

Something we can't begin to understand. Even God said we can't comprehend it in Proverbs 30:18–19:

> *There are three things which are too wonderful for me,*
>   *Yes, four which I do not understand:*
> *The way of an eagle in the air,*
>   *The way of a serpent on a rock,*
> *The way of a ship in the midst of the sea,*
>   and the way of a man with a virgin.

Think about that for a minute. What could be so mysterious and incomprehensible about an in-love male-female relationship? It happens every day. You don't have to go far to find two people who are newly in love.

It's not the rarity of the occurrence that makes it amazing, it's the incomparableness. This inexplicable connection is uniquely theirs. A one-of-a-kind bond. As he kisses her and she kisses him back they create their own magic. In fact, I might go so far as to say no one is a bad kisser, they just haven't made the right match yet. It's all about finding the ideal combination.

That's what I'm waiting for. Someone who makes my heart skip, my stomach drop, and my body tingle. And I'm not talking about indigestion.

Yes, I want—as Olivia Newton-John put it not-so delicately—to get physical but, when it comes right down to it, a one-night stand isn't good enough.

Will a one-time hookup truly understand me, heart and soul? Will he laugh at my jokes? Will he know when I'm nervous? Happy? Scared?

Or, if I gave in and we happened to meet again later, would I wonder if he's thinking, "Yeah, I nailed that." Sorry for the crudity but I think that's about as romantic as you're going to get with a one-nighter. Is it really worth risking your heart over?

Flip the Switch

Anyone who knows me knows I struggle with my weight. It's been an ongoing problem since I was a college freshman. Much of the time it makes me feel unattractive and unlovable. Over the years, I've gone back and forth between wondering if I'm still single because of my size and fearing no one would want me even if I were thin. As a matter of fact, I have lost weight and looked good for significant periods of time, but, no, my dating life didn't change. Losing thirty pounds did not prove to be the hoped-for magic elixir that drew men to me.

My youngest sister used to have her own weight issues. Then, one day, her mind switched and, ever since, she has been committed to diet and regular exercise. She dropped to a healthy, attractive weight and, for the most part, stayed there. This change happened around the time of a very significant incident in her life. How much the two are connected is hard to know, but it triggered something in her that had a lasting impact.

Which makes me wonder what my trigger might be. To tell you the truth, I've often felt love and intimacy would be a lovely replacement for food. I'm pretty sure it would be a smooth transition since it seems I eat my loneliness and repressed passion. Wouldn't it be great if the one thing you want the most had the power to slay one of your worst demons? Yeah, I know. Wishful thinking.

In the meantime, I live in the hope there's a guy out there who'll like me anyway. Then I become my own worst enemy. Why would any halfway decent man be interested in goofy, old me? He'd have to be a loser, right? And I don't want to date a loser. Even if, at the same time, I wonder if I'm good enough for him. Ack! It's enough to drive someone crazy. No wonder I'm constantly beating myself up. It doesn't make sense. I don't make sense.

Sigh.

Anyway, I was talking about replacing chocolate with sex. Seriously, that's what I was saying. I just suspect that if I was getting a little something physical I wouldn't think about food quite so much. Maybe that sounds a bit naïve. Since I have so little experience in the matter, I'm mostly speculating. Intimacy has been, for the most part, nonexistent in my life while good ol' Hershey has always been there for me. Unless I run out. But then it's just a quick run to the store and, voila! ... satisfaction.

Contrary to popular opinion, women do think about sex, and I'm no exception. We struggle with temptation. We have, as they say, needs.

Okay, so, what are our options here? We've already discussed taking "personal" time, which leads to guilt. If masturbation is something you struggle with, it's a "habit" worth overcoming.

God, in His wisdom, only gave us one legitimate outlet for sexual expression and that's between a husband and wife within the confines of marriage. We might not like it but since He's the one who created sex He should be the one to make the rules. And we not only hurt ourselves when we don't follow those rules, we're in danger of causing harm to others too.

It's time to ignore what society pushes on us because here's the fact, Jack: God expects us to reserve those thoughts and feelings for marriage. This will not, I repeat *not*, be easy. We can't just snap our fingers and make those thoughts and feelings go away. They have to go somewhere. But I'm learning that just because something is hard doesn't mean God will give us a pass on it.

I have to remind myself that God knows so much more about what's going on than I ever will. What if I had met up with that Brendan-Frasier-cutie-who-was-married so many years ago? Though I can't *know* what would have happened, I can make a few assessments: This man was not in love with me and nothing we might have done would have changed that. When I found out he was married (and a father) a few days later, I would have been humiliated and devastated. I would have never been able to go back and change what I'd done. And I would have regretted it for the rest of my life.

Just a few things God knew then that I didn't figure out until much later. He protected me despite my foolishness and ignorance.

Though God created us as sexual beings, He expects us to be in control. So I choose to bury my desire in ice cream and peanut butter cups and nachos with cheese. (Which is a whole different kind of lack of control but, fortunately, this isn't a diet book.) Other people fill their lives with busy-ness or exercise or work. But, let's be honest, sometimes we replace what we're missing with sin. We become adept at excusing it too:

It's so difficult, God. You have no idea how hard it is! I'm surrounded by sex. Just five minutes of TV and I'm thinking about kissing, which can lead to thoughts of a lot more. You said it's better to marry than to burn, Lord. Well, I'm burning! And you won't let me marry ... so what am I supposed to do?!

You ask too much.

Wow. Did I really write that? Is that how I feel?

Would I be so brazen, so arrogant as to tell God Almighty where the lines will be drawn? This requires disregarding everything I know He's done for me, including giving His Son to be brutally crucified and to bear my sins so I might spend eternity with Him.

Whenever I tempt myself with thoughts of what I could get away with I run full force into God's love for me and how much I owe Him. I want to ignore it, but I can't. Though I should find comfort in that love—and often do—it also binds me with guilt. Guilt I bring on myself, continuing this rollercoaster of what I should do, what I shouldn't do, and the emotions that tear me up one mountainside and down the other.

And then, just as I'm wondering what on earth is wrong with me, I remember Romans 7:15–24:

> *For what I am doing, I do not understand. For what I will to do, that I do not practice; but what I hate, that I do. If, then, I do what I will not to do, I agree with the law that it is good. But now, it is no longer I who do it, but sin that dwells in me. For I know that in me (that is, in my flesh) nothing good dwells; for to will is present with me, but how to perform what is good I do not find. For the good that I will to do, I do not do; but the evil I will not to do, that I practice. Now if I do what I will not to do, it is no longer I who do it, but sin that dwells in me.*
>
> *I find then a law, that evil is present with me, the one who wills to do good. For I delight in the law of God according to the inward man. But I see another law in my members, warring against the law of my mind, and bringing me into captivity to the law of sin which is in my members.*

> *O wretched man that I am! Who will deliver me from this body of death?*

I know exactly how he feels. I know how quickly you can get to that point where you want to tear out your hair in frustration. But here's the truth of the matter: We all fail. We all let God down.

But, thankfully, that isn't the end of the story. Paul adds: "I thank God—through Jesus Christ our Lord! So then, with the mind I myself serve the law of God, but with the flesh the law of sin."

Once again we see that God rescues us, this time from ourselves. Yet we are still trapped by our sinful flesh. We don't give up, though, because, by God's grace, Paul then comes to a grand conclusion as the discourse continues in chapter eight:

> *There is therefore now no condemnation to those who are in Christ Jesus, who do not walk according to the flesh, but according to the Spirit. For the law of the Spirit of life in Christ Jesus has made me free from the law of sin and death.*

Forgiveness followed by freedom. That just might be the best antidote to guilt.

God doesn't deal in fairness but in holiness. My life exists for His glory, not for my happiness. If my singleness brings honor to Him, then I should strive to excel in the life He's given me and find my happiness there. God has called me to obedience no matter what that looks like.

It won't be easy, but I choose to believe I'm up for the challenge.

Story of Hope—Kris

As a young adult I had many romantic relationships. From the time I started dating at fourteen through my late twenties, I was my own black book. There were very few weekends I didn't have someone to go out with. My value of who I was slowly had become what men thought of me. It would eventually cause many bad choices and much heartbreak.

I got to the point where I didn't know if guys were dating me because of me or just what I looked like. Yes, I was hot back then. I had a voluptuous shape, long blonde hair, and the personality to go with it. Despite how I looked, though, I was obsessed with having a boyfriend during the holidays so I wouldn't be alone. Even if I didn't like a guy that much I would go out with him anyway. I had this insatiable hunger for wholeness and value. I didn't know it at the time but what I was missing was the Lord. He would be the only one who could truly fill me and make me whole.

During my college years, I accepted Christ, attended church, and participated in a Bible study, which I eventually helped lead. But my relationship with God was mechanical. Do this and He will give you this. Do that and He won't strike you down. Yes, I was being filled by God now but at what cost? My life was so legalistic. I switched from trying to please a man to trying to please the man. A path that would also lead to the destruction of my mind. You cannot work yourself to heaven. So I would fall away, back into the lost world and, again, make horrible choices.

The only difference was now God would convict me because I had accepted Him into my life. I just lacked the right church and right discipleship to help me grow. After college I moved in with a new boyfriend, to the shock of family and friends. This guy had also recently accepted Christ. We felt if we lived together like a married couple then God would be okay with it. At least we weren't sleeping around.

Please know God does not bless sin. Even though I was in love (to the best I knew of it) and enjoyed my time with this man, God kept whispering to me that I was His and this relationship was wrong. He had bought me with the price of His own blood, His own death on the cross. And He was the only one who could fill me—not this man I was living with—and make me whole and bring value to my life.

I would eventually leave that boyfriend and wander another year, searching for something, anything, moving from this relationship to that relationship until finally I waved the white flag to God. I just couldn't do it anymore. My way was not the right way. I realized I needed Him.

That's when things changed. I found a church and a group of Christian friends struggling the same way I was. We helped each other. God forgave me and restored me. He is that kind of God.

Nothing I had done or ever could do was beyond His forgiveness. I was chosen by God, His child forevermore, never to be alone again. Never to have to find my value in things or people. Now I find my freedom in my relationship with Him.

"Restore to me the joy of your salvation and grant me a willing spirit, to sustain me" (Psalm 51:12, NIV).

Kris Swiatocho
Director of TheSinglesNetwork.org Ministries
Garner, NC

Now, It's Your Turn

- How do you deal with sexual temptation? What could you do differently?

- How do you handle wanting to feel desirable while still staying pure before God?

- If you have fallen into sexual sin in the past, what, if anything, have you done to break free? Do you feel forgiven? What is your relationship with God like now?

- Which of the verses referenced in this chapter stood out to you the most? Why?

- Do you suspect you bring some of the guilt on yourself? In what way(s)?

- What are some of the negative things you say to yourself that hurt your self-esteem? How can you turn those negatives into something more positive? What Scriptures can you find to help you do that?

- What are some sacrifices you feel you should make in order to keep your mind—and body—pure? Are you willing to do so? If not, what's holding you back?

Chapter 7

Anger
Love Is a Battlefield

When angry, count four; when very angry, swear.
—Mark Twain

The anger I felt toward God over my persistent singletary state was, for the longest time, one of my more consistent emotions. It seemed He, more than anyone, could actually do something about it. He's all powerful, almighty God. If there was a "right man" out there, somewhere, for me—and I still choose to believe there is—God alone knew where he was and, of course, where I was, and He could have brought us together.

If He wanted to.

And therein, quoth Shakespeare, lies the rub. Why didn't He want to? If I had a dime for every time I asked that question, I could have hired Paris Hilton to walk my dog.

Just kidding. I don't have a dog.

Most of my achingly single friends, though reluctant to admit it, are angry at God. When a man-less woman refuses to go to someone else's wedding—putting her own disappointment above the happiness of a friend or, even, a family member—that girl is so mad she can barely move. Sure, that anger comes out in tears, and she would claim sorrow (not anger), but those tears are like waves of electricity just before lightning strikes. I'm speaking mostly about women here since, in my experience, men don't particularly like going to weddings anyway, married or single, because, well, it's just not a guy thing.

Of course at my age, I've witnessed many a friend begin our acquaintance single then skip out of it happily wed. Yes, I sometimes struggle not to get too Oscar-the-Grouch-like while, at the same time, fighting off the temptation to imagine what my own day will be like. I've made an effort to not take the Grouch or the Daydreamer with me. This day is about the two people walking down the aisle. I choose to rejoice with them. It's not about me. Heaven forbid my disappointed hopes should ruin someone else's love ceremony!

Besides, I've never gone to a wedding where I felt the bride was gliding toward a man meant to be mine. I suppose it's possible, but it hasn't happened yet. Why can't I celebrate the hopeful future they are pursuing so passionately while eating their food and, potentially, meeting their single guy friends? That's why I go and if, for whatever reason, it gets me down—especially as the age difference between me and those young blushing brides grows wider and wider—I deal with it. Good grief, I've been doing that for more than thirty years.

Ouch. Did you hear that? Anger. Frustration. And a pinch of self-pity. That little comment is a good example of what I'm talking about. The anger is always close, just under the surface, skulking there like the Hulk, waiting for enough provocation to turn me into something monstrous. Mostly, it makes its presence known through little things—like when I have to kill spiders or when I long for a shoulder massage or when I really want sex and there is simply no outlet for it. And if I'm not strong enough to lift, move, or open something, I'm just plumb out of luck.

I've discovered being single so long turns us into

loners, if we weren't already wired that way. Though I'm an extrovert by nature, over the years I've come to love being alone. At times I even look forward to it, especially after a busy day.

But that's not necessarily a good thing. Not when I stumble home and collapse into solitary nothingness. My backside has a far too personal relationship with my couch and the TV has become my way of escaping the quiet of a two-bedroom house that only sleeps one. Though I try to fill my days as much as I can, I tell myself I need my downtime. And for singles, downtime equals alone time. So I scroll through Facebook while watching romantic movies, and try not to think about how angry I am at God.

That's how *I* handle it, but there are variations ... we're all different. Some women completely swamp their lives with activity. The more we do, the less time we have to think about the way things are. But whether we're doing everything or nothing at all, we're only throwing a quilt over the anger. It's a way to distract our minds and try to forget how many times we've prayed that prayer, wept our grief, and begged for answers we never seem to get. Just push the anger aside until tomorrow. Then, when we do think about it, it's easier to resign ourselves to our lot in life and slip into a woe-is-me pity party with the underlying anger always hovering right beneath the surface.

"What's the point?" we say. "It's obvious God doesn't care."

That, my friends, is our quiet, frustrated dig at God. And even if you have the presence of mind to remind yourself of all the evidence you have that proves how much He loves you, it's not enough. Because if He does care but, for whatever reason, remains quiet, that silence still slices and dices its way through our hearts. How could continued silence feel like anything but apathy? And it's this overwhelming sense of indifference from the One we've come to believe loves us the most that twists the dagger into our gut.

Still, we try to remain faithful. So we turn to prayer as our singular hope. *God, it hurts. You know it does. I have to believe You love me. And yet, this deafening quiet.*

If you've seen the movie *Amadeus*, you probably remember the scene where Salieri turns against God. All he claims he ever wanted was to serve God through music. When he sees Mozart—an uncouth, vile, blasphemous child with an innate gift for musical genius that Salieri can only dream about—he reacts with an intense anger bordering on hatred.

"So be it!" he cries out. "From now on we are enemies, You and I."

Many of us have felt that way—even if only for a moment. And I don't like it. I don't like anything that makes me feel separated from God. Yet the potential to react like Salieri is there, rapping at my skull with wicked-sharp fists.

Are you sure God loves you?

Yes, in my heart and soul, I *know* He does. But I am only human and the doubts come and the thought that He could love me and still not care about my lonely, grief-soaked heart drags me down to an angry place and anchors me there far more often than I would like.

How could it be that God loves me … yet no man on earth could? This question would burst out of me in tearful screams, when I was driving in my car or lying in bed in the middle of the night, or even in a room full of friends, where I had to bite my lip and pretend I got something in my eye. I never felt the anger with the finality of Salieri, but always with equal passion.

Fortunately, God can take it. And though He didn't always comfort me in those times like I wished He would—and He rarely responded—I still felt safe enough, loved enough, to be angry. Angry enough to spit, yell, stomp my feet, and shake my fists. Angry enough to feel abandoned by God.

Hopeful enough to never give up hope.

Who Said Life Is Fair?

Many years ago, I spent time with a woman who liked to party, drink, and sleep around. Who cheated on her husband and was, when we met, pregnant with another man's child. Months later, she got a divorce, gave birth to a beautiful baby, and, eventually, married the father.

I, on the other hand, spent most of the first five decades of my life wanting a family but thinking if I was patient enough and trusted God and believed His best was my best then this perfectly legitimate desire would, one day, be fulfilled.

Yes, I knew God never promised me marriage or children. For the longest time, I thought He did. It never occurred to me He hadn't included those roles in my life story. Instead, throughout my forties, my bitter, broken heart wondered if He even cared. My advancing age seemed to mock my hopes as the ability to have children moved toward its inevitable end. At one point, I realized I will very likely have to take a menopause test without ever needing a pregnancy one.

And this made me angry.

Though I can't recall the original source, a friend once

told me a childless woman going through menopause is experiencing the death of all her children. How could I not feel grief-anger at the thought? I didn't want to think God would purposefully put me through this. But why not? Why should I be immune? Why shouldn't I feel pain?

The day after my fifty-first birthday, I "celebrated" by having some dental work done, including an extraction. An excruciating extraction. As the dentist tugged and pushed and worked that poor dead tooth root, deep pangs shot through my skull. Each time, I tried to pull away and moaned. I'd mumble, "I- hur" ("It hurts" in dental patient dialect), then add, "I- o-ay," ("It's okay.") because I didn't want more Novocain. But she gave me more anyway, until the numbness seeped right up to my eye.

And it still hurt.

As I lay there wondering if I should groan again because it hurt so much, the thought hit me: "Why shouldn't I feel pain?" I didn't take good enough care of my teeth and now I had to have something that should be permanent yanked from my skull and that's gonna sting. Maybe, I thought, I should just yank up my big girl pants and deal with it.

We live in a society where we don't want to hurt—physically or emotionally. I go to a lot of effort to avoid painful situations. And I kind of expect God to be a part of that. Since He loves me, He should protect me from anything that will injure me. And that includes the injury to my heart over my continued singleness.

I want Him to fix what makes me sad and when He doesn't, I don't get it. Shouldn't love equal happiness? Or is there something I could do to make the hurt go away? This is my first-world mindset at work—wanting my life to be easy and fun and full of chocolate and flowers because

I've managed to convince myself I deserve it.

But why shouldn't I be sad? Why shouldn't I go through tough times? Why shouldn't I feel pain? And why can't I focus more on all the blessings in my life instead of constantly wanting, even expecting, more? All of which leads to anger when things don't go the way I would like them to.

An end to my hope for children has to be close. My period is still surprisingly regular but some months it shows up late. And, in my youth, I was rarely late. I keep better track of it than I used to, noticing subtle changes, wondering each month if the flow will end and the hot flashes will begin.

One of those first really late months happened the same week I met the aforementioned party girl. Guess that's what got me going, anger-wise. I was trying to be obedient and she just wanted to have fun. *I'm dying inside*, I thought, *and God is creating life in her.*

Then there are all those young married women who are just not sure if they want to have kids. At least not yet. Oh, they might say, what's the rush?

"We just want to enjoy the two of us for now." Or even, "Children are a lot of responsibility. But we have a dog and that's enough!"

To which I smile politely. And cringe inside. *Well, isn't that special.* All I need is a dog. Or a cat. And some knitting needles. Then my life would be complete.

What's funny-sad is I know many of the right answers to my anger issues. I grew up in the church. I am aware of the errors expressed here. What right do I have to be angry at God? As noted earlier, God never promised us *fair*. In fact, He often goes out of His way to make sure we know fairness has nothing to do with anything.

Take the book of Hebrews, for instance, where the writer spends all of chapter eleven describing these amazing heroes of the faith of whom, he concludes, "the world was not worthy." Men and women who followed God without question and, often, to death. And yet they, "having obtained a good testimony through faith, did not receive the promise, God having provided something better for us, that they should not be made perfect apart from us" (11:39–40).

What this says to me is, these people served God without question and with their lives and, because of that, He made them a promise. But they won't see the fulfillment of that promise until we're all together. He did this to provide something better—not for them, but for *us*.

It's not "fair" to them, but it is merciful to us.

And one of Jesus's parables clearly states that God's idea of fair is far different from ours. He tells of a landowner who hired men to work his vineyard, then paid the same to those who worked one hour as those who worked all day. When the day-long workers complained about the lack of equality, the landowner said,

"Am I not allowed to do what I choose with what belongs to me? Or do you begrudge my generosity?"

Then Jesus adds, "So the last will be first, and the first last" (Matt. 20:15–16, ESV).

Okay, so maybe God isn't swayed by my pleas for fairness. But understanding that didn't help. It didn't make me less angry. Or more willing to end my woe-is-me weep-fests. That said, I never wanted to reach the place where, like Salieri, I couldn't forgive God for my situation. I wanted things to be better. I wanted *Him* to make things better.

When He didn't, I felt abandoned, even forgotten. I'm

not sure there's anything worse than feeling like God doesn't care. And, I discovered, that was just a hop, skip, and a jump from anger. That's where I found myself: lonely and childless, wondering if I was even lovable. Clinging to God's Word and His promises. Not perfect but wanting to be better. Striving to follow the will of God so He would be pleased with me. Feeling like a failure and questioning everything.

God help me, but no matter how hard I clung to Him, the whole thing still made me angry. How I wished it didn't! How I wished I were one of those women who relished her singleness or loved her career or had accepted it all with strength and courage. In my weakness I felt, at times, overcome with resentment. I had to fight the concern that God had dealt falsely with me.

Back when I was still in my thirties, I felt called to participate in a one-month semi-fast. Each day, I made the commitment to not eat until 6 p.m. and, instead of lunching on peanut butter sandwiches or beef vegetable soup, I would spend that time in prayer and Bible study. Specifically, I hoped to determine God's will for my life with regard to marriage and a family. Despite my eagerness for both, I wanted to be open to His plan, whatever it might be, even if it meant singleness. By the end of that month, however, I believed God told me quite clearly that He not only had marriage in store for me but it would happen within a year.

Obviously, I was wrong. And it broke my heart. To think that after a month of focused, fervent, and delighted time with my Savior, truly believing we had communicated and He had spoken to me directly, the year that followed ticked by without even a hint of a relationship. I now know I was mistaken. Whatever God said to me during that month slipped right by. I misunderstood. Or, more likely, I simply created the response I wanted.

Perhaps I was wrong to have marriage be the reason for the fast, yet at the time I thought the matter was important enough to make it a priority, and I believed God would want me to bring it to Him. After all, the desire was *from* Him. He was already involved.

So, what happened? It's been well over a decade and I feel further from marriage than ever. How could I have been that wrong? This question haunted me ... and I had to work through the anger I felt not only toward God but toward myself.

In many ways, I know this was my fault. I wanted to believe He was telling me what I most longed to hear. Like I said, it was quite possible I created my own prayer-conversations during that time. I do have a gift for dialog. In fact, at the time of the fast I wrote scripts for a living. My ache was so great—what if I imagined those beautiful words of comfort and encouragement and promise?

Over time, I came to realize I needed to rely on Scripture because those are the words I *know* are His. But I can't just read the words, verse by verse, chapter by chapter; I must trust God to speak to me through the Bible and then be open to *all* He has to say. Even if it's not what I want to hear.

Anger Toward Others

> *Don't hold to anger, hurt, or pain.*
> *They steal your energy and keep you from love.*
> — Leo Buscaglia

I'll admit I'm a bit of a Facebook junkie. I love the connections I've made, the friendships that have been strengthened, and the gradual advantage it has been to my career. I've also seen the dark side of Facebook ... and it isn't pretty.

It started innocently enough. A friend posted something silly on her wall. One of her male friends—someone I don't know—remarked, "You are so funny! How are you still single?!" That made me laugh and I couldn't resist replying, "If men wanted funny, I'd know a lot fewer single women."

This stranger, who, it would seem, doesn't share my sense of humor, responded, "I take it you're single, *Ms.* Kopf. By the way, your bitter is showing."

Ouch. Clearly a response to this insensitive ... person was warranted but where would I start? When I made the comment, I was not motivated by any bitter feelings; I just wanted to be funny.

Sure, I believed there was some truth to what I wrote, but I don't think I was being mean about it. Men aren't necessarily beating down the doors to date witty women. A sense of humor can be a must-have for a lot of girls when it comes to liking a man, but, in my experience, it's not high on the list for most guys. That's okay with me. It's just the way we're wired.

But instead of seeing my words as a humorous commentary on the differences between men and women, he disagreed with me. This, too, was fine. My problem with the whole dialog was his decision to attack me personally about it in one of the cruelest ways possible. I imagine he knew that to deride a woman's singleness while accusing her of being bitter had to hurt.

As you can probably guess, we did not become

friends—on Facebook or otherwise.

So we've established the fact that this man's comment was hurtful, rude, and unnecessary. But was it true? Dear God, had I really become *that* girl? That ... *spinster*? In some ways, and on certain days, I realize I have. When I snap at someone about being single, especially men, there's bitterness oozing out. I'm kidding myself if I think they don't sense it, even feel it.

Talk about a wall.

Our hearts have been broken in an incredibly painful way. Lifelong desires have been thwarted, often without reason or cause. Not knowing how to respond to the pain, we lash out. It's a bitterness born of grief, something you don't just decide, one day, you're fine with. These things take time. Another reason we need to let ourselves mourn.

It's nice to see, though, that God gets it. "Hope deferred makes the heart sick," Solomon wrote in Proverbs 13:12.

But is that what I am? Heartsick? Did years of disappointed hopes and frustrated dreams turn me into a bitter old maid?

I wish I could say it didn't get that bad but, some days, it really did. I would hear myself berate someone or say something mean, and I knew where it came from. Too bad all they heard was the anger, the frustration, the bitterness.

If only I could scoop up the words with my fingers and shove them back down my throat before anyone had a chance to hear them. I couldn't, of course, and the ache of my loneliness would creep out in hurtful comments I would often immediately regret. Then I got to watch as people scurried away.

"No, I'm not angry at you," I'd say to their hastily retreating backsides. "What I meant to say was—" but it was too late. And I realized I blew it. Again. *Keep it to yourself, Sharyn. You can't say something mean if you don't say anything at all.*

I *wanted* to be a better, kinder person. But the years kept trudging by and I could feel the bitterness rooting itself deep into my soul and I didn't know how to dig it out. Could I expect a man to come along and help by taking a shovel to it? Would I want one to? Not really.

And yet, if the bitterness and anger buried in my heart was because of my spinsterness, perhaps he—whoever *he* is—*could* help. Maybe all of it could be taken care of by having the right guy in my life.

Now if you're thinking, "You should find your hope in Christ alone," I agree, in many respects. And, for the most part, I rest in that knowledge. He is my strength, especially on the tough days. Even if, unfortunately, I sometimes forget to turn to Him. I wish I was the kind of person who would faithfully stand on hope despite her circumstances, always confident in her relationship with her Lord. If only my far-too-human heart would stop getting in the way. Because, as I've pointed out, what I'm asking for is a good thing. The first relationship God created was between a husband and wife so, clearly, He considers it an important one. Why not hope for the blessing myself?

That's just the first of many questions. Asking questions in small doses is a natural part of life. Sometimes we get answers; sometimes we don't. We expect that.

It's the wait that starts to get under our skin. Feeling hope fall apart after years and years of what feels like God's silence scratches at our romantic dreams. When we wake up each morning to a cold, lonely reality—and we're not sure why—how can it not get more and more difficult to fight off the frustration and, yes, the anger? Our life is not right ... and we feel powerless to fix it.

Sadly, though, when it comes to grieving singleness, anger isn't the worst stop on the way to hope. We have one more pain to deal with. Bear with me, dear friends, because in my experience nothing strangles hope like the next stage of grief.

Story of Hope—Joanne

I stood at the end of her bed, crying. Just minutes ago, as I leaned my head against my mother, she had breathed her last breath—a long, slow sigh I will never forget. Now other family members were hugging her, all of us engulfed in sorrow's shock. As grief tightened around my heart, a gut-wrenching realization flooded in: I'll never get to shop for a wedding dress with my mother.

Not that I was engaged or even dating at the time. Not that I had ever really dated. I was almost thirty-eight, and getting married was becoming the impossible dream. I had already been single longer than I'd ever expected to be. It felt extra cruel that while I waited for God to provide a husband, He allowed my beloved mother to die. If God did answer both of our prayers for my future husband, I would never be able to share my joy with her.

Later that awful day, my entire family packed into the coroner's office. I couldn't help but notice that each of my three sisters had the arm of a boyfriend or husband around her as we discussed our mother's burial. If ever I longed for the loving arms of a husband, it was then. Never had I felt so uniquely alone.

Early in my grieving, I turned to Psalm 23 because I didn't know what else to read. I had plunged into the valley of the shadow of death, as verse four says. I didn't want to face life without my mom, and I feared depression. But when I read the next phrase, "I will fear no evil," it seemed to promise I did not need to be afraid that would happen.

Over the next year, I felt overwhelmingly sad. My heart was broken. After another year and a half, right after I turned forty, depression crept over me. While some things began to feel normal again, I noticed a short-temperedness in myself that hadn't been there before, an over-sensitivity I thought I'd grown out of years before. My normal motivation to stay disciplined with my schedule, exercise, and eating habits waned. Beneath the sadness, a sharp edge I couldn't quite identify stabbed against me.

Someone once said that depression is anger turned inward. It wasn't until I sat with a counselor that I began to identify that sharp edge as anger. And I was angry. Angry that I had to grieve my mother alone. Angry that my church community hadn't done more to reach out to me during the time I needed them most. Angry that many women dreaded things like making wedding plans with their mothers when I would never get to do that with mine. Beneath the deep hurt in my heart, I suppose I was angry at God for allowing me to remain single when He was the one who designed marriage in the first place.

I expected to talk a lot about grief with my counselor. Instead, our conversations focused on helping me identify the reasons why I felt angry in certain scenarios. As I pondered those issues, I also finished a book I'd been writing for many years about singleness. I focused on resolving my emotions while writing my story. And I studied God's sovereignty and tried to figure out how He viewed long-term singleness.

Right after I completed the manuscript, my counselor asked me an important question: "Have you ever told the Lord you'd be okay if you never got married or became a mother?"

"No," I said, a bit shame-faced.

"I think it's time for you to have that conversation."

Knowing he was right, I prayed earnestly in the car as soon as I left his office. Although my feelings didn't immediately match my words, my heart was sincere. I realized I hadn't fully done the very thing I'd written about: let go of the life that hadn't happened and take hold of the life He had planned. I asked the Lord to help me do that, and to give me a new dream for the next season of my life.

Since then, my life has changed. I still don't understand why my mother had to leave us so soon, but God has answered her prayers for my husband. Not long after my prayer of surrender, the handsome man I'd been eyeing at my biweekly small group from church asked me out, and the rest is history.

The weeks leading up to my wedding were very emotional for me as I thought about my mother. I missed her deeply, but I no longer felt angry. I was overwhelmed with joy on my wedding day, and I'd like to think that my mom was rejoicing with me in heaven, if God allowed her to know what was happening to her daughter on earth.

Joanne Chantelau Hofmeister
Writer
Franklin, TN

Now, It's Your Turn

- What sets off your anger about singleness? How do you deal with it?

- Do you think it's okay to hope for marriage? Is it possible to want a husband yet still be content in your relationship with Christ?

- Have you become bitter? Or do you worry you will? What do you do about it, if anything?

- If you don't think of yourself as a bitter spinster, are you still concerned that others might see you that way? Why or why not?

- Do you find yourself putting on an act of being happier in your singleness than you actually feel? If so, what can you do to make that happiness more real?

- How has your singleness affected your relationship with God? Has it drawn you closer? Made it harder to trust Him? Caused you to question His love for you? Or do you simply try not to think about it?

Chapter 8

Depression
Open Arms

Jesus has a very special love for you.
As for me, the silence and the emptiness is so great
that I look and do not see, listen and do not hear.
—Mother Theresa

One day while still in my thirties and living in Colorado, I stopped at the grocery store to grab some milk before heading home. As I rushed down the aisle that seemed to lead most directly to the dairy section, I was suddenly assaulted by the scent of baby powder and diapers. I skidded to a halt and stood there for a moment, stunned. Something so sweet, and yet it assaulted me like a vicious right hook. This unexpected reminder of the empty ache inside of me struck at my longing for children of my own.

It wasn't the first time I had recognized this desire but it was the first time I realized it might never happen. In that moment, I grasped how quickly I was approaching an age when it would no longer be possible. Though I knew I still could have children, time was running out ... and the truth of my situation struck me with all the force of a category five hurricane. Fear, shock, regret, anger, and hopelessness pounded my heart like waves. I plunged, temporarily, into an ocean of grief, right there in the middle of Albertson's grocery store.

Yes, I clawed my way out and finished my errand, but

the waves still beat against me to this day. So I do what I must to keep from drowning in the grief.

Almost two decades have passed since that night, and from then on I made an effort to steer clear of the "baby aisle" whenever possible. If I can't avoid it because of a baby shower, birthday, or Christmas presents, I have to mentally prepare myself. For years that meant hardening my heart and refusing to think about it, which didn't seem like much of an improvement over the anguish. I certainly didn't want to lose my desire for a family and, in doing so, give up a part of myself. I already felt as if the womanly, motherly side of me was being slowly suffocated by neglect.

C.S. Lewis wrote:

> *To love at all is to be vulnerable. Love anything, and your heart will certainly be wrung and possibly broken. If you want to make sure of keeping it intact, you must give your heart to no one, not even to an animal. Wrap it carefully round with hobbies and little luxuries; avoid all entanglements; lock it up safe in the casket or coffin of your selfishness. But in that casket—safe, dark, motionless, airless—it will change. It will not be broken; it will become unbreakable, impenetrable, irredeemable* (The Four Loves).

It would be so easy to retreat inside myself, to not offer anyone any part of me, to remain safe and secure, untouched and untouchable. But though I don't want my heart to be safe and, as a result, turn to stone, for so long I didn't know what I could do to prevent that from happening. Either I lived in the midst of my grief or I hardened my heart and ignored it.

The grief would hit me one minute and I'd start to fall apart, but before the pain got too unbearable, I'd push it away, thinking I'd deal with it later. "Later" is a funny thing, though. Because "later" never comes, and the passing of years not only made the grief harder to handle, but harder to ignore. And always on the horizon lurked menopause like a cruel killer, waiting to put a brutal and bloody end to my dream of children and a family. I still don't know how I'll handle menopause, so I don't think about it. Instead, I've decided God will prepare me when the time comes.

On the other hand, I see the wisdom of getting my heart ready now. How do you prepare yourself for something like that? One day at a time, I suppose. But I'll write more about that later.

Back in my forties, though, everything about the situation frustrated me: the desire that wouldn't go away, the knowledge of just how quickly my time was running out, and the inability to do anything about it. I felt completely helpless. Sure, I could adopt or try artificial insemination. Yet that would mean raising a child without a father, which wasn't what I wanted either. Someday I may change my mind about adoption; for now, it doesn't seem to be a wise decision. And so, all I had left were fragments of hope whispering the possibility that, somehow, it wasn't too late for me.

Fragmented hope, however, can only get you so far. Not long after the grocery store incident, I was at a routine doctor's visit when I mentioned, in passing, how much I wanted to have children and how I believed God was keeping my eggs safe for His timing.

"Oh no," the doctor said, shaking his head in what I

can only call a momentary lapse in empathy, "they're going down like the Titanic."

That was, oh, about fifteen years ago.

But Not For Me

Every once in a while, I read another one of "those" stories and, more often than not, it gets to me. And not in a good way. I don't want it to. I realize these accounts are told to offer encouragement and hope. So, yes, some guilt weaves its way through my emotional reaction, and then I start crying. I'll stick to the basic details since I'm pretty sure you've heard something similar before and will start to track with me fairly soon.

Two young people meet, date, have sex, and, what do you know, she gets pregnant. A difficult situation to be sure. In many accounts, they're quite young. What to do?

Her family members might push her toward an abortion, many even insisting they should not get married, claiming that would only ruin three lives. The young couple struggles with their sin, asks God for forgiveness, decide to marry, and, soon after, give birth to a beautiful, bouncing (I assume), baby boy. Or girl.

God graciously and lovingly not only forgives their sin and disobedience, He creates something beautiful out of it. No indication they were lonely, but He puts them in a family anyway.

In Psalm 68:6, David wrote, "God sets the lonely in families …" (NIV). I've clung to that idea for years, praying it would, one day, be true for me. "I'm lonely, God. Please put me in a family."

The wait I went through made me that much more

aware of these happy endings. Though I don't understand how God decides these things, I haven't held a grudge against anyone who's struggled because of bad choices. By His grace, though, I've came to a place of forgiveness and healing. It's a beautiful place … but it took me forever to find it.

Instead, I spent the better part of my life struggling with this perceived sense of unfairness.

"It's not right, God," I'd whine. "For over thirty years, I've ignored my sex drive, my loneliness, and my desire for children, all in an attempt—okay, so maybe not to perfection (as we saw in the guilt chapter), but I did sacrifice to follow Your commands and wait, as You seemed to want me to do. I believed my dreams of a family revolved around obedience to You in this matter and if I did my part, You would do Yours."

So I waited, and each year that waiting got harder. Though I tried to be patient, God's silence made it even more difficult. The quiet engulfed me. Gave me a lot of time to think. And the thinking led to questions.

Why did I sacrifice?

What had I waited for all those years? To find myself facing menopause without ever knowing the joy of having children of my own? To see the wrinkles on my face and hands, to feel the pain of aging in my back and knees and know I wasn't as capable of caring for a child as I once was? To wonder if, had I given in to temptation years ago, I might have become a wife and mother, secure in her Father's forgiveness … not this lonely spinster who felt abandoned by God?

I've had to accept the truth that even *if* I meet someone and even if I meet him soon, and *if* by some miracle I get pregnant, the possibility of carrying a healthy child to term is incredibly slim. One statistic stated that not only does a woman over forty have a mere 1 to 3 percent chance of conceiving, the advanced age puts the baby at a higher risk for severe, even deadly, birth defects. The mother is in danger of problems as well.

On the other hand, the *Discovery Health* TV station aired a special years ago about a woman who gave birth to her first child at the age of fifty-five—a healthy, eight-pound boy. Though stories like that gave me hope, I worried that wasn't necessarily a good thing. At some point I had to accept the truth of biology. God can do anything—I certainly believe that is true—but was it wise to cling to a dream that could only be fulfilled by a miracle?

Ignore the ache. Stop whining about what you don't have and be content with what you do.

But we all know it's not that simple. As I've said before, this desire is perfectly natural. God created women to want intimacy, love, and children. Family. In my common sense moments (I do have a few) I realized it wasn't God's will for me. Not yet anyway. I hoped it was. For so long I hoped with every optimistic bone in me.

One day, my romantic heart believed, God would take me by the shoulders and turn me around. There, standing in front of me, would be him—the man He'd chosen for me.

"See?" He'd whisper. "I told you it would be worth the wait."

Someday.

If only I could see the future I could prepare myself for whatever lies ahead. I could handle, maybe even enjoy, the wait. But, as we know, life doesn't work that way.

Take, for instance, my unfortunate fear of flying.

(Hang in there, I do have a point.) Unfortunate because I actually love the sensation of soaring miles above the earth. I like the speed and the height and am amazed I live in a time when a single woman at my income level has such an opportunity. It's not something I take for granted.

Nevertheless, I am aware of how out of control I am. If something happens in that plane and/or to that plane, well, there's nothing I can do about it. So I freak out, questioning every bump, wondering what that sound meant or why it feels like we're slowing down.

Should we be slowing down? Now we're speeding up again! What is that pilot doing up there?!

Yeah, I don't handle it very well. I have to keep reminding myself to relax, that my life is in God's hands and He loves me. I have, I can sheepishly admit, always made it to my destination safe and sound. I tell myself that, perhaps, I should just enjoy the ride unless there's an actual, real reason to worry. You know, like we're plummeting to earth or the landing gear has fallen off or the plane is hit by a really big bird. If only I could have known everything would be fine, I could have appreciated the experience so much more.

It would be so easy to trust God with my longing for children if I knew how my story would end. I'd be able to relax in peace or accept the inevitable with grace. But I *don't* know. All I know is the laws of reproduction are not on my side. My biological clock went off years ago and I've been desperately hitting the snooze button ever since.

And God knows I'm running out of time.

Rejected...

I had a dream once where I was in a hotel, wandering from room to room, looking for someone I wanted. But each door I came to only slammed shut in my face. Finally, I collapsed in a heap in a cavernous, warehouse-like room as I fought the tears.

Then I tried to kill an orange spider that morphed into a green flying wasp-like thing that came after me.

Hey, it was a dream.

When I woke up I felt rejected. And a little freaked out about being stung by creepy, orange-green, flying spider-wasps. Anyway, as a single woman in her fifties who's never been in a serious relationship, I have, for all intents and purposes, been rejected by men my whole life. I've been rejected in my career, too—set aside twice, as previously noted, and snubbed by a number of potential employers and editors and agents for years.

Oh, sure, a few men have asked me out and the companies I've worked for appreciated my creativity. Over the years, several editors have expressed interest in my manuscripts and requested to see more and told me how good and lovely and even necessary my work was ... and still turned it down.

Please understand my purpose in sharing this is not to invite you to feel sorry for me. I don't regret the bad times. God used each and every rejection to strengthen me and make me the woman and writer He created me to be. But when we go through those periods of rejection—and we all do—it's how we come out of them that matters most.

And if I hadn't gone through them, I wouldn't be able to relate to others who've experienced similar disappointments. Who doesn't want to be pursued and desired and needed? We come into this world, arms outstretched, screaming for love and attention. Then we spend a lifetime learning just how painful that need can be when it's ignored. Eventually, we discover:

We're attractive ... but not enough.

We're interesting ... but not enough.

We're talented ... but not enough.

So we bear with the rejection time after time while wondering how much a person can take before she completely breaks down.

"Please love me," we beg, arms still open wide. "Let me be good enough!"

I've felt that desperation of wanting to be wanted. It's usually about that time when I realize what truly terrifies me: Maybe God has rejected me too. Maybe men don't want me and employers don't want me because God doesn't want me.

And, once again, I wonder, am I unlovable?

Isn't it easy to go there? So simple to drop our hearts into a cistern of grief and, yes, self-pity.

"You should have told me, God," I would say, stomping my foot and scowling. "You should have told me You wouldn't give me what I want without reason or cause.

"You should have warned me I'd be on my own."

But, perhaps, He did warn me. In the middle of John 16:33 (NIV), Jesus said, "In this world you will have trouble. ..."

That's not the whole verse, thank God, but we'll get back to it later.

... *And Abandoned*

It's perfectly natural that we would feel this loss and wonder if God has abandoned us. Scripture is chockfull of people who felt the same way, including Jesus Himself:

"And about the ninth hour Jesus cried out with a loud voice, saying, 'Eli, Eli, lama sabachthani?' that is, 'My God, My God, why have You forsaken Me?'" (Matt. 27:46).

"When my prayers returned to me unanswered, I went about mourning as though for my friend or brother. I bowed my head in grief as though weeping for my mother" (Psalm 35:13b-14, NIV).

And, of course, there's poor, abandoned Job. In chapter six, verse eight of his book he cries out, "Oh, that I might have my request, that God would grant me the thing that I long for!" Three chapters later, he says, "For He crushes me with a tempest, and multiplies my wounds without cause."

By chapter thirty his despair is clear: "I cry out to You, but You do not answer me; I stand up and You regard me, but You have become cruel to me; with the strength of Your hand You oppose me."

Throughout the Psalms, like Job here, the writers beg God to hear their prayers and to not be silent. That's where our biggest problem lies, isn't it? Not in the worry that God has abandoned us or that He doesn't love us or that He wants us to be miserable, but in His silence. His patient, maddening, stick-a-fork-in-my-eye silence.

"Just say something, God. Anything."

Who hasn't said that? It's why I fasted so many years ago. To break God's silence and, finally, hear His answer.

But we can't make God talk any more than He can

make us listen.

Because here's the thing: While working on this book and reading the Bible and thinking through all of it, I realized I've spent a lot of time waiting and wanting to hear some kind of audible, even supernatural, response from God and not nearly enough time absorbing what He'd already told me in Scripture.

What has He told us? I suppose exploring that would fill a book on its own. Instead of trying to cover everything, I'd like to take a deeper look at our friend, Job. When I read his story several things strike me as similar to my own struggles, though mine are certainly not on the same scale.

First of all, Job didn't understand why he was suffering. Though he refused to "curse God and die" as his wife suggested, he had questions. He and his friends then spent thirty-four chapters hashing it out. Reading through his dialog reminds me so much of my own thoughts and prayers and frustrations. He begs, he excuses, he reminds his friends—or himself?—who God is and what He's promised.

Second, he's hurting. How could he not be? Forget about the loss of money and land—all ten of his children are dead. The only person left is his grieving, bitter wife. You can feel his pain: "My destruction from God is a terror to me, and because of His magnificence I cannot endure" (31:23). Beautiful and poetic and heartbreaking, isn't it?

Then, after almost forty chapters of discourse between Job and his four friends, God finally shows up. He speaks out of a whirlwind. But here's what gets me: Does He offer comfort and understanding? Does He answer Job's questions? Does He give this aching, human heart any kind of consolation?

Nope.

He yells at him. He challenges him as a man. He mocks his pain. And then He goes into a pages-long discourse on ... animals.

For so long, I didn't get it. How could God be so heartless to someone who loved Him? To someone He described as "a blameless and upright man, one who fears God and shuns evil," so much so that there was "none like him on the earth" (1:8)?

Not only did God describe Job that way twice, but the second time He added, "And still he holds fast to his integrity, although you (Satan) incited Me against him, to destroy him *without cause*" (2:3—*emphasis mine*).

"Without cause"—the same words Job used in chapter nine. Job's pain and confusion and grief were legit. He'd done everything right. He was a good man. But God allowed all of this to happen and then, when Job needed His compassion and understanding the most, God berated and degraded him.

What was I missing here? There had to be an explanation; God doesn't do anything without reason. After God finishes His monologue, we come to chapter 42, where Job speaks for the first time in more than ten chapters. He doesn't seem upset, though certainly browbeaten and humbled. Two things he said stand out to me: That he had spoken of things he didn't understand and that he had only heard of God before but now he had seen Him.

This leads him to say, "I abhor myself, and repent in dust and ashes."

Taking all of this into consideration, we can come to a few conclusions:

One—we're in way over our heads. We cannot even begin to understand God or His plans and we certainly can't see the big picture like He can.

And two—God is God, we are His creation, and He works in our lives according to His will and for His glory. We might never understand, but …

God loves us anyway. In his final speech, Job says, "I know that You can do everything, and that no purpose of Yours can be withheld from You."

I had to get to the place where I trusted God no matter what. Where, even on the days when my arms ached to hold someone, I could still believe He loves me. Even in His silence. And as I've turned to Him the bouts of depression have lessened as my faith has increased.

Not only that, but God has brought laughter, joy, and, yes, children into my life.

You Come Back

God has blessed me with some amazing nieces and nephews. I adore those kids and, in 2013, I had the opportunity to move to the same town as three of them, which means I get to see Katy, Lucy, and Oliver at least once a week. And every time I walk through their door, they hug me, they're happy to see me, and, often, have something to show me.

I smile a lot.

Oliver is a funny, crazy kid who is always into something. And, for the most part, he's very independent. Or at least he wants to be. But when he was three, Ollie started experiencing separation anxiety. Up until then he'd handled being dropped off at childcare without any trouble. But something happened and, suddenly, he couldn't take it. He would scream and cling to my sister, Susie, like she was heading off to war.

Ever since I moved closer to my family, Susie and I have tried to work out at the YMCA a few times a week. And, until this *don't-leave-me* phase, Ollie spent that hour happily playing with the other kids. Sometimes, he even talked his mom into going when she didn't feel like it.

Then everything changed. And before you say, "Well, just leave him. Soon he'll settle down and start playing and be fine," let me add that if Susie did that—just walked away—he didn't only cry. He threw up. And that wasn't something she wanted to do to the nice staff at the Y.

So we stopped going. (Yeah, I should have gone anyway, but that's another subject.)

My nephew soon indicated it wasn't just his parents he wanted to keep close. I'm over at their house on a weekly basis and, around that same time, he started running up to me as I was getting ready to leave, saying, "You come back, Aunt Sharyn. You come back."

These words had a surprising impact on my single heart. Being near my sister and her children was *the* reason I moved from Colorado to Ohio in 2006. I needed that sense of home and family. Every time I hug those kids it is like perfume to my soul.

As much as I loved Colorado, being so far from family just got more and more difficult. I missed them all so much, I could definitely relate to Oliver's desperation to keep his loved ones close.

Earlier I mentioned the verse in Psalm 68 where King David sang about how "God sets the lonely in families." When God opened the doors for me to move to Ohio, that's exactly what He did. Now my separation anxiety can be remedied with a five-minute drive.

This has been so good for me and my grieving heart. Though I don't have children of my own, God has put several in my life and it has made all the difference. In the next chapter, I'll say a little more about this.

Still, I realize it's not the same. When I heard there was a new Cinderella movie releasing in March 2015, I couldn't wait to see it with the kids. I was so excited, I felt like a kid myself. But the family went one afternoon while in another town and told me about it later. They enjoy doing special, just-them activities that I'm not a part of. And that's okay. Most families do. But that's a loss for me because I don't have a husband and children of my own. I have a hard time imagining special family times without them, but theirs don't automatically include me. Understanding why it's that way doesn't make it easier to handle.

It's a tough topic, this idea of grieving our childlessness, knowing God may never tell us why and we have to accept it. But though I may not have all the answers, this I do know:

In Him I place my hope.

Story of Hope—Tammie

When I was in high school, many years ago, I imagined a grown-up life that included an early marriage to a loving husband and six kids. Never in my wildest dreams did I see myself single into my forties.

As my sisters and friends got pregnant and had babies, I struggled with feelings of inadequacy and sadness. It was hard to watch others experiencing their greatest joy while waiting for my turn. As the years passed, I slowly let go of my dream children one by one.

First it was, "So, it's okay to have only five kids," and it was easy to put the depression I felt aside. Then I downgraded to four. With each passing year, the sadness and depression deepened and it took longer for me to break free of it. As I approached my mid-forties, I came to realize I wasn't meant to be a mother to my own biological children.

Then, during one of the toughest years of my life, God revealed to me that He had heard my dream. And although it wasn't part of His plan for me to be a mother, He did provide me with the opportunity to experience some of the nurturing and joy of having children. Instead of six children of my own, God blessed me with six nieces and nephews. Even better, my youngest sister, her husband, and their two children live half a mile from me. She has shared her life with me in an incredible way.

Teresa's husband, a Marine, was in Afghanistan while she was pregnant with their youngest. They weren't sure he would be back in time for the delivery, so they asked me to be her labor coach. I gladly accepted the role.

She called me when the baby was squeezing her so tight she couldn't breathe. She told me about the nights she had to sleep sitting up. I accompanied her and her older child to the ultrasound that revealed the gender of the baby. And I was there the morning the false alarm took us to the hospital at 5:30.

When the delivery time came, I sat with Teresa all day. Later, I cut the cord and placed that precious little one in his daddy's arms for the first time.

Over the years, I have experienced **Barney, The Wiggles, Guitar Hero,** *and* **Dance, Dance Revolution.** *I have picked up kids at daycare and stayed with them when they were sick and Mom had to work. I have been soccer mom and taxi service. I have attended musicals, back-to-school nights, birthday parties, karate practices, the orthodontist, and soccer games. I've given them a ride when they missed the bus or dropped off the art supplies forgot.*

Overnight visits have allowed Mom and Dad to get away for a night, a weekend, or even a week. I know the joy of waking up beside the warm body that sprawled across the bed and kicked me all night. I grin when I think of seeing that smiling two-year-old face first thing in the morning, saying, "Hi, Tammie!"

I have been a horsey and a pillow and a mean lion. I have bouncy-bounced on the trampoline, and been laughed at when I fell down and couldn't get back up again. I have played games, read stories, and kissed hurts away.

God had a plan for me that didn't include children of my own, but it did allow me to experience the joys that parents do. My sister is an amazing mother and she has shared her two wonderful children with me. I have four other nieces and nephews and I regret that I haven't been able to live close enough to share these things with all of them. But I have never regretted the time spent helping my sister when she needed me.

I have lived vicariously!

Tamara D. Fickas
Second-grade Girls Pioneer Club Teacher and Aunt
Colorado Springs, CO

Now, It's Your Turn

- Have you yet reached a point where you can accept God's will for your singleness or are you still struggling to come to terms with it? Write out how you feel about this.

- Do you have moments of deep sorrow because of your singleness and/or childlessness? If so, what brings you comfort?

- Have you ever been depressed to the point of needing counseling? Did you go to a counselor and, if you did, what was the result?

- Has your depression ever made you consider suicide? What stopped you?

If you are currently struggling with thoughts of suicide, I encourage you to contact a supportive friend or loved one and openly and honestly share your heart. Don't keep it inside! And if you don't have someone who fits that description, you are more than welcome to contact me. Even if you simply want someone to pray with you.

Consider finding a licensed counselor as well. The American Association of Christian Counselors offers you access to approximately 50,000 state licensed, certified, and/or properly credentialed Christian counselors. Their website is www.aacc.net.

Focus on the Family has on-staff counselors you can call for a free consultation at 1-800-A-Family (232-6459) Monday through Friday between 6:00 a.m. and

8:00 p.m. Mountain time. Also, Focus's website provides a form you can fill out to find a counselor in your area.

- Do you have a support system—a group of friends who understand your grief and provide comfort and a listening ear? What do you talk about with them? What helpful advice have they given you? If you do not have this, please let me know!

Chapter 9

Hope

(Everything I Do) I Do It For You

Hope deferred makes the heart sick ...
—Proverbs 13:12a

This book wasn't easy to write. I'd be clipping along at a good pace, then the accusations would sneak up on me:

You're not qualified. You don't have any answers. How could you, when you're just as confused and hurt and frustrated as ever?

So I would put my notebook away for a while.

But, inevitably, something hit me—an epiphany, a truth, a Bible verse—or I woke up in the middle of the night sobbing, the ache coming from a place so deep I had forgotten it was there until it struck. And the only way to work through any of it was to put pen to paper and pour everything into words on pages.

I've mentioned my deepest fear—that God just doesn't care. In the movie *Impromptu*, author George Sand studies a painting by her friend, artist Eugene Delacroix. In it, a tiger seems intent on taking a rather large bite out of a young woman's side.

George says, "She doesn't seem bothered she's being eaten alive. She'd probably say, 'Better to feel something than nothing.'"

It is better. It has to be. Better to feel God is angry with me than to fear He never thinks of me. I'd rather cry from the depths of a broken heart than never know what it's like to love someone deeply.

I want to *feel* my life, even if it hurts.

Words

At the end of the day, and especially at the end of a long, lonely night, I knew God loved me. *Because the Bible tells me so.* But do you remember in *My Fair Lady* when love-smitten Freddie woos Eliza by dreamily crooning his passion for her? He starts babbling something about birds and how his heart tumbles and heaven crumbles because of her when, suddenly, Eliza, interrupts.

"Words, words, words," she says in last-straw frustration, "I'm so sick of words!"

Then she passionately proceeds to tell the confused but eager boy to, basically, shut up, take her in his arms, and *show* her how he feels.

In retrospect, though, it was really *my* words I was tired of hearing. The excuses, the accusations, the pity parties and even, to my shame, the prayers. I'm not ashamed of the fact that I prayed, but I felt unsatisfied. It seemed as if the prayers hit the ceiling and bounced back at me.

I didn't want to ask God for a husband anymore because it had gotten to the point where the words seemed empty and meaningless. God knew how I felt. I'd certainly mentioned it plenty of times. But, even more, He gave me this desire. He knew it wasn't going to disappear without some divine intervention. So unless He did something to help, I didn't see those feelings fading away anytime soon.

Then there was the fear He was just as tired of my words as I was. Sometimes it seemed like we were both taking a step back, waiting for the other to do something. I knew He knew what I wanted from Him. What kept me up at night was figuring out what God wanted from me.

Yes, I say that like I had no idea. But I did know. He wanted my obedience. He wanted my devotion. He wanted me to fear Him and to pursue a pure heart. And, for whatever reason, He wanted me single and, as far as a husband was concerned, waiting. Without a clue as to how long that wait might be and what it was for.

Still, *how* He told me to wait made it not sound so bad. In fact, He offered hope:

"Wait on the Lord; Be of good courage, And He shall strengthen your heart; Wait, I say, on the Lord" (Psalm 27:14).

Isn't it our hearts that are at risk here and the most in need of hope? How comforting to know God recognizes the courage it takes to wait when everything inside us screams for action. I can't possibly know what my future holds and, for the most part, I'm sure I'm better off *not* knowing. The hope I cling to can't revolve around a man but around God. We need to be aware of and reminded of the gifts He offers us, especially during the tough days.

For me, one of those gifts might seem a bit silly, but I now have a different perspective on love songs. Because I don't have a man in my life, I often interpret romantic lyrics to reflect God's feelings for me. Even cheesy pop tunes can remind me just how much I mean to Him.

Yes, I know that's not the purpose of these songs and, usually, not all the words fit into the "single for God" perspective. Still, you can find gems of truth in many of them.

Like the Bryan Adams song I used as the subtitle for this chapter: "(Everything I Do) I Do It for You," that includes the lyrics, "I'd fight for you ... walk the wire for you ... I'd die for you." (Yes, I passed over the line about lying.)

Peter Gabriel's "In Your Eyes" works so well as a Christian song that Nichole Nordeman did her own cover of it in 2002.

A few years ago another little song trumpeted the affirmation that the right guy will see his girl as beautiful and incredible and unforgettable without any care as to how others see her. He'll discover in her everything he ever wanted.

I think it's safe to believe God feels this way about me.

Silly, emotional, messed-up me.

Taking it a step further, Psalm 18:19b says, "He delivered me because He delighted in me."

So, here's the question: If the One who holds the universe in His hand and who sacrificed His only Son for my eternal joy *delights* in me, why do I need anything more?

Well, it might have something to do with the fact that I don't think I'm good enough. What could He possibly see in me? I'm inadequate, selfish, unworthy. If I don't think I'm good enough for a man made of earth and water, how can I be worthy of The One who breathed into the mud and created life out of nothing?

Perhaps I can start by believing what He says is true. Beginning with the fact that He delivered me—another translation says "rescued"—because *He delighted in me.*

Silly, emotional, messed-up me.

I heard once that if you repeat a truth often enough you'll eventually believe it. So maybe if I keep saying it over and over at some point my insecurity and low self-esteem will be quieted, allowing the words to sink in.

"Jesus loves me, this I know." A simple children's

song, but I encourage you to capture it and hold it in your head and heart.

The love He has for you is *alive* and true and unconditional and never-ending.

Soak that up like a hot bath with plenty of bubbles.

Take a Chance on Love

It's surprising how often I'm not only a witness to but a participant in a developing romance between friends. Maybe it shouldn't surprise me, but it does. As I wrote this section, I watched as two beautiful friends step-danced their way through the intricacies of love. I saw it all from her perspective as she wondered just how interested he was. Since she was my roommate at the time, I listened to her concerns and offered my thoughts. Mostly pointing out how often he texted and, occasionally, called her, and his creativity in finding reasons to spend time with her.

"Trust me," I said. "Though I don't know a lot about men, I do know he wouldn't be doing any of that if he didn't like you. Seriously like you." And, it turned out, he really did.

In fact, it was all rather sweet and I loved watching their romance bloom. Of course, being the hopeful romantic I am, every once in a while during those uncertain weeks as they tried to figure things out, I found myself crying, just a little, because I was so happy for them.

But I also cried a few months into their exploratory relationship when it seemed he wasn't going to take a chance on love. I couldn't understand why anyone would let fear or uncertainty or anything, really, get in the way of something with the potential to be so wonderful.

Especially since the possibility of love in my own life felt further and further out of reach. I haven't given up the dream of meeting someone, and, when I do meet him—I say optimistically—I hope I'm not the kind of person who runs away from love, whether out of fear or anger or high expectations or whatever.

Anyway, back to my friends. They worked through it and were married less than a year later. One night after they got engaged, I wanted to tell her how delighted I was for them but I couldn't say it without crying and I had to write it down. I can't *not* be a romantic. I can't *not* hope the best for those I love. And I can't begrudge their happiness because of my own disappointed hopes.

Why can't we share the joy of love-fulfilled for our friends and family? Our dreams for romance don't have to be limited to our own lives. So many people are lonely, lost, aching for someone to reach out and help them up.

Whether we're making a match between two good friends or babysitting for parents in need of a date night or volunteering to help an elderly neighbor mow her lawn, giving of ourselves—our time and our hearts—meets a need, even if it doesn't involve fevered kisses under the moonlight. I want to wish good things for other people, not just for myself.

Though I'm not there yet, I'm working on it—working on becoming a better version of myself. And, while I'm at it, I might as well hope that elderly neighbor has a single son my age.

Cause and Effect

I love romance novels. And romantic movies. Anything that ends with a kiss and the promise of a walk down the aisle stirs my senses and makes me smile. I can't help it. I'd put a fantasy-inducing kissing scene in this book if I thought I could get away with it. But since this is my story and I have yet to enjoy a decent smooch, I'll leave that particular fiction for my novels.

Anyway, I've often been warned by well-meaning friends to avoid the gooey-kissy hearts and flowers stuff—anything dripping with romance that makes me long for something that is, today anyway, still out of reach.

But I'm not sure that's the problem. I didn't become a romantic by reading *Pride and Prejudice* three times; I read *Pride and Prejudice* three times *because* I'm a romantic. I don't want someone to kiss me because watching *Spider-Man* (2002) kiss Mary Jane while he dangled upside-down from a web made me feel like Cirque du Soleil was rehearsing in my belly. That kiss made my stomach flip because I want someone to lay one on me, and I hadn't realized until then that the upside-down thing was such an intriguing notion.

Let's not get the cause and effect confused here. I'm a romantic by nature. Do these books and movies make it worse? How could they? My desire for love and a husband is innate. As I've said, I can't let go of the hope that it could still happen.

If anything, those thoughts and longings are worse about once a month, and anytime I can't find chocolate when I need it. If the first, I swallow a few Advil and watch a favorite movie. Not necessarily a romance. I might be more in the mood for *Iron Man* or one of the *Lord of the*

Rings films or a classic like *Rear Window*. If the chocolate is an issue, well, I just do what I can to make sure I always have some somewhere. Which is its own separate problem because it means I'm eating and ignoring my emotions rather than dealing with them.

I wish I could say I've always turned to God while going through a rough spot, but I can't. He hasn't been constantly at the forefront of my mind like He should have been. I'm too easily distracted—by what I want and what I don't have and the anticipation that something might still happen. And when I did look to Him, the nagging fear that He wasn't going to do anything held me back. I didn't want to be turned down again. Especially since His "no" usually came through silence, and the simple fact that nothing had changed.

Here's the crazy way my brain works: As time went by, I became more and more hesitant to look to God, afraid of more silence. If I didn't ask, I decided, I wouldn't feel rejected as my singleness continued.

This is where the problem truly lies: I can turn to books and movies and chocolate in times of grief but not to God. He should be my first thought. I've spent years trying to break this barrier in my mind. It's one built of fear, self-absorption, and a lack of trust. I don't like feeling separated from God.

I had to figure out how to trust Him despite not getting what I wanted. But how would I get to the point where He's my *only* hope?

Believe it or not, I found that answer while writing my novel, also titled *Spinstered*. More on that in a bit.

Hope Without Hope

I've experienced His Presence in the deepest darkest hell that men can create ... I have tested the promises of the Bible, and believe me, you can count on them.
— Corrie ten Boom

Even now, with the breakthroughs I've experienced, I have days when I don't feel particularly hopeful. Yet here I am, writing about it anyway. Still, don't you need hope the most when it's hard to remember how it felt? As much as I want to be a positive thinker, I don't want to sit here in denial, refusing to face facts.

For so long, my hope centered around the belief that, one day, Prince Charming would gallop into my life. That would still be lovely, don't get me wrong, but it can't be the purpose or point of hope.

When I sense God asking me what I really hope for my first thought is marriage and a family, obviously. But is it? After all I've been through—most of which I've shared in this book—that seems the most logical answer. Of course that's what I want. Yet when I look past the romantic dreams of my heart to the desperate longings of my soul I realize what I truly long for is a life with purpose—one that brings glory to God, whatever shape or marital status that comes in. Hand-in-hand with this is the recognition that His plan for my life may not include a wedding or children. His answer to my question might continue to be "no." I had to decide if I could live with that.

I wish I could respond with the faith and trust the virgin Mary showed when Gabriel told her God's intention: "Behold the maidservant of the Lord!" she said. "Let it be to me according to Your word" (Luke 1:38).

If only. Instead my "yes" comes hesitantly, with caveats:

"Yes, Lord, I'm all right with never marrying if You will be here for me. If You will take the desire away. If You will give my life meaning."

It's not the same. It means He's not enough. I'm still trying to find my hope in Him ... plus something more.

If I am to pursue a life that brings glory to God it can't be about me or a husband or a successful career. Or children or weight loss or my house or my family. Strip it all away and I would hope to find a willing and obedient heart beating strong in this hurting, confused dreamer. A heart that's a little cracked and slightly bent but not broken.

When God called me to write a nonfiction book about singleness a few years ago, He asked me to share the grief side of the unmarried life, which inherently includes some things I never intended to tell anyone, except maybe my sisters and a close friend or two. Then, at the beginning of the process, it occurred to me this might be the reason God wanted me to wait on marriage. This book would never have come to be if my matrimonial dream had come true.

I had to ask myself, "Am I okay with this? Can I thank God and worship Him wholeheartedly if He has denied me a husband and children so that I could, *would* write a book about grieving singleness after forty? Even knowing that to do so would mean exposing my pain and sorrow, my hopes and dreams and, yes, my sin and mistakes to whomever would choose to read it?"

Sure, it was nice to have a possible reason after years

of asking God why I was still single. Yet I had to answer this question before I could move forward. And, honestly, it didn't take long. I knew the answer was "yes." Writing is my passion and I believed I had things God wanted me to say about over-forty spinsterhood.

That said, I also know if I were to go back in time to my twenties and ask myself, "Sharyn, would you rather marry and have children now or stay single and barren so you can write a book that would minister to women dealing with those issues?" I would have chosen a family any day of the week and twice on Sunday. I would have believed God would find other ways for me to serve Him. And I would have been right. I can't thwart God's plans, free will or no.

That's not how it worked out, though, and I found myself saying, "Yes, Lord, I will rejoice in my singleness and follow Your will no matter what."

And then I thought, "Wait a minute. How can I do this? I'm such a mess, how could I possibly help anyone else?"

To which He replied, "My grace is sufficient for you, for My power is made perfect in weakness" (2 Cor. 12:9a).

Which begs the question: Will I be able, one day, to respond as Paul did in the rest of that verse when he wrote, "Therefore most gladly I will rather boast in my infirmities (in my case, weaknesses), that the power of Christ may rest upon me"?

Dear Lord, I sure hope so.

Back-door Hope

I've mentioned the difficulties I faced the first time I was laid off while living in Colorado, which eventually led me to move to Ohio. Ten months passed after I hauled all my stuff to the Columbus area before I finally landed another full-time job, this time as a public relations/marketing writer for a small Christian university. Though I enjoyed the work, always in the back of my head was the fear it wouldn't last. I didn't feel a great deal of job security.

Sure enough, in January 2010, I was called into my boss's office and given the devastating yet too-familiar news. It wasn't as bad as the first time because I was a little more prepared, mentally, but I still left the building in tears. You can never be emotionally ready for something like that.

For the first few nights, that voice telling me what a failure I was pounded through my mind. I balked at the idea of having to start the job search process all over again. Money—or the lack thereof—would quickly become an issue. I'd been stretching it to cover my rent as it was in my pretty, spacious, sun-filled, and far-too expensive apartment.

Everything crashed down around me, and I was scared.

These thoughts seized me by the throat in the days following the job loss. And yet, in the midst of the heartache, there beat a measure of hope. It was small and I had to dig for it, but it was definitely there.

One morning I woke up with the words from the Third Day song "Call My Name" singing through my mind. Specifically, the lines urging me to call on God, never doubting His deep, abiding love for me. So, I did. There in my bed, I cried out to my forever Father, asking Him to give me hope.

He reminded me of His love, and then, to my surprise, He offered me the gift of time. As a writer with numerous projects shrieking to be completed, time was a precious commodity. When I was committed to a full-time writing and editing job, I had scant motivation to go home and sit down at another keyboard to work on my personal projects.

Just like that, I no longer had such an excuse. Besides, since I'd asked God to find a way for me finish this book, several novels, a few scripts, and even a screenplay or two, should I really be so despondent and ready to give up on life when He had done precisely that? Sure, His ways aren't my ways, but that's a good thing. As someone who depends on surprise in her craft, perhaps I should be grateful for His unusual tactics.

In other words, sometimes hope is found in retrospect.

Finding Hope In Broken Dreams

Speaking of hope found, let's go back to the novel version of *Spinstered* I mentioned a few pages ago. Now, the thought had occurred to me more than once that I should try to turn this concept into a novel. I've always thought of myself as a fiction writer. Indeed, a romance novelist. But though I tried several times to start a novel, it just never felt right.

Until one day when a character named Catie—a forty-eight-year-old never-been-married career girl—introduced herself and her friends to me. Just like that I had my story, and I went to work. I combined my heartache with an Ohio friend's actual romance for the plot. Suddenly things seemed to be moving forward—I even had a publishing contract for a short time.

And I thought, "This is it. This is why I'm still single."

Because through all of my grieving singleness I was constantly looking for a reason. I needed there to be a purpose for my brokenness. There had to be a story to tell to make it all worthwhile. Yes, my grief over my perpetual singleness was still hard but if I could minister to others through it, or become a stronger person, or, at least, come to appreciate how much better it is to be single than in a bad marriage, I'd finally have a reason I could understand.

At the end of my novel, Catie has a similar experience. She feels abandoned and alone and she wants to know why. She decides to do what she loves to do—go for a hike. Since she lives in Colorado Springs, good trails are everywhere. This is what happens:

◊◊◊

I bundle up in my warmest quilted parka, plus a hat, scarf, and gloves, hoping to ward off temps in the low twenties. At least there's no wind, but it's still frigid-cold. I move quickly. It's the best way to warm up.

Once I reach the top of Mount Cutler, I simply stand there, taking a moment to catch my breath and admire the view. This would be a good time to pray. I'm alone up here. I have so much to say, I'm not even sure where to start.

Flecks of snow start to drift around me. I probably should head back down soon. Instead, I hike a little farther across the summit. Trip over a tree root. Stumble. And twist my ankle.

"Really, God?" I say, out loud. And that lets loose the torrent. I can't stop yelling. About everything. I'm glad I'm alone and no one can see me, screeching to the heavens, tears streaking down my face and mingling with flakes of snow.

But I'm angry. At God. And guilt joins hands with the anger. I shouldn't be mad at God for this situation, especially since so much of it is of my own making. Yet if anyone could do something about it, that would be God and, still, all I feel is His silence. Years of silence.

"Has any of it ever been real?" Then I scream, "Where are You? What do You want from me?"

And a still, quiet voice whispers, You, Catie. I just want you. But can you just want Me?

I do just want you.

No, you don't. You want what I can get for you.

The words hit me like a Mack truck. I stumble to my knees, my heart breaking more than it ever has. He's right. All the time I've wasted longing for something instead of God. I can tell myself over and over how what I've wanted was a good thing based on a desire He gave me but, in the end, I placed marriage as my ultimate prize and God as the horse I would ride to win it.

And now, I've been whacked in the face with what I've lost—the time I could have spent basking in Him, enjoying His love and presence rather than moping and whining and asking God why He hated me so much. Was it hate that yearned to know me without anyone else getting in the way? Was it hate that gave me so many years to come to know Him intimately?

"God, You are the prize, the goal," I whisper into the cold snow whipping around my head. "You didn't let a husband get in the way of that. But I did. Even though I didn't have one, I let him come between us. A fantasy of my own making."

Then, because it has to be said, I add, "Please forgive me. And please take me back."

A silly thing to say, of course, considering I left Him.

When I stand up, my ankle feels surprisingly better. I'm able to hike back to my car without any trouble, knowing I'm not alone.

◇◇◇

The point is: We should never see God as the provider of the dream. He *is* the dream. That's it.

Publishing my books has been a dream come true—even though, in the end, I had to do it myself. On the other hand, I am—like Catie—more single today than I have ever been. There isn't even someone on the horizon. I haven't been head-over-heels attracted to a man since Mr. Wonderful. Does that hurt? You bet. I'm human, a woman, and, as previously mentioned, a hopeless romantic, to boot. But it's okay because my greatest dream has already come true—God loves me and I belong to Him. And if I want to truly find hope that has to be enough.

We need to stop making our faith about what God can do *for* us. Our hope is found in what we do for *Him*. That's the reason. And that's my second big lesson about being single.

Seven Reasons Singles Should Cultivate Relationships with Kids

Every once in a while, I step outside my regular writing genre and try something else. Like the time I felt inspired to write a children's book. It's something I've always imagined doing, mostly because I thought it would be fun. The inspiration was, surprisingly, an annoying little summer cold I came down with a few days before. While sniffing, sneezing, snorting, and a-chooing, it hit me kids would probably enjoy those words in a book. And that's how *Tricia Mae Is Sick Today* was born.

Something like this would not have happened, I'm sure, if I it weren't for the relationships I have with children. So when I chatted with a woman recently who doesn't have any youngsters in her life, it struck me how much she was missing … and how grateful I am for these relationships.

All of which led me to come up with the following list of reasons singles should have children as a regular part of their lives:

1. **They offer unconditional love—**

    In fact, I would say kids *want* to love you. They start out willing to give you a chance to be someone they care about. It's up to you to take that chance. As for me, I know my nieces and nephew love me no matter what I say or do. And they know I adore them and would never hurt them.

2. **No one can hug you like a child will—**

Melt-into-you, nothing-held-back hugs that make everything seem better. Trust me. When you're having a bad day—and even when you're not—improve your mood with a hug from a little one.

3. **They keep you young at heart—**

On Labor Day one year, my oldest niece and two of her friends decided they wanted to make a movie about three schoolgirls who are kidnapped, escape into the woods, and stumble upon a strange group of "frog people" who help them find their way home. So the adults put on funny costumes and made funny faces for a funny little movie our families will always cherish.

4. **They inspire your imagination—**

From giving me ideas for characters and plots in my work to inspiring me to dress up in a crazy costume at a moment's notice, I stay on my toes, creativity-wise, thanks to the kids in my life. They certainly make me consider things I never would have otherwise.

5. **Children forgive and forget easily—**

   While shopping at a souvenir store on vacation one summer, my nine-year-old niece skipped up and asked if I'd give her five dollars. She was adorable, but I was distracted and said no. Just like that. Later I felt horrible for being so dismissive, and I apologized. She smiled sweetly and said, "That's okay!" before bouncing off again. She didn't hold a grudge. Her feelings weren't hurt. She loved me just the same as always.

6. **You can pass things on to them, even if you're not their mother—**

   Having someone to leave a legacy to was a concern before I became an aunt. Now I would love to have something to leave these wonderful children. And, I believe, they'll be there for me should I need help when I'm older.

7. **They give you hope—**

   Children don't give up easily, and they don't think you should either. They believe in you. Their perception of life and all its potential hasn't yet been tainted by harsh realities or great loss or broken hearts. Kids make you feel better about all that life still has to offer.

If you don't have nephews and nieces, there are other opportunities to foster relationships with kids. Become a Big Sister. Teach a Sunday school class, like my friend and fellow writer, Tammie. Another single author I know is godmother to a good friend's daughter.

Be a volleyball coach, direct a kid's play, invite a group of students to your house for a cookout, or get together with other singles and offer the parents at your church a free night of babysitting.

Give a little of yourself and you'll be amazed and delighted by all you get in return.

Hope Delayed

In chapter six, I wrote about a semi-fast I took several years ago. The one where I spent thirty days in close, focused communion with God, and, at the end of the month, felt His assurance that I would marry. Not only that, but I would meet "him"—the man He intended for me—within the year. And I told you that, looking back, I felt betrayed by God. How could I have been so wrong? I even wondered what the point of it all had been.

A decade or so later, I finally grasped the only explanation that mattered: I had enjoyed a month of intimate fellowship with my Savior. Wasn't that reason enough? Didn't I love those days, and don't I cherish the memory still? Yes, I came to a wrong conclusion. I'm not sure why, but I'm certain my tunnel vision toward husband-hunting had something to do with it.

I know now it was worth it, and I continue to reap the benefits of those thirty days. How could I not? It meant so much to me that the next year I tried a forty-day semi-fast—again only eating after 6 at night and spending my lunch hour in prayer and Bible study, journaling my thoughts and memorizing Scripture.

This time, I didn't get any epiphanies about a man, but I did know God loved me and had a purpose for my life. I just needed to be patient. I needed to trust Him.

Today, I look back on that time, and I'm grateful. It meant something to me; surely it meant something to God too. Whenever I feel lonely or abandoned or afraid, I can remember the beauty of those weeks with Him and know it was real. As V. Raymond Edman said,

"Never doubt in the dark what God told you in the light."

Hope for Today

> ... *But* when *the desire comes, it is a tree of life.*
> —Proverbs 13:12

I often think about the first half of this verse in relation to my singleness: "Hope deferred makes the heart sick ..." It's so wonderful to know God doesn't leave us there. That's only half of the verse. Best of all, He says, "*when* the desire comes," not *if*.

He has your heart. You are safe. The bad days last but a season—something everyone must go through, married or single. Your grief is not sin. You don't have to stop wanting to marry. Whether it happens for you or me doesn't change or diminish God's love for us.

Now here is my conclusion, such as it is: I honestly don't know if I will ever stop grieving my singleness. Not completely anyway. But I can say the tear-filled nights are fewer and further between. The ache has lessened to a degree, though that doesn't mean it won't, occasionally, grip my heart in loss and loneliness.

My desire for children finds a home in the lives of my nieces and nephews. I cherish this opportunity to live just a few miles away from my youngest sister and her three kids. They hug me, kiss my cheek, tell me stories, and make me laugh. We spend birthdays and holidays together, and I go over there almost every Sunday there's a new episode of *Once Upon a Time* on so we can watch it together. I introduced my nieces to the *Anne of Green Gables* TV mini-series and they loved it as much as I do. And my nephew is a burst of energy that is like electric shock treatment to my heart. In a good way.

I love spending time with my sister, and, since my dad lives on the same farm as she and her family, I've enjoyed a chance to develop a stronger relationship with him as well. On the downside, I haven't made many friends in the area yet and, as far as I can tell, there aren't any single men within a fifty-mile radius. Still, I'm content. Frustrated, lonely, freaked-out, happy, loved, and content.

Perhaps God will one day say "yes" to my prayer and bring a man into my life. Or the sense of peace and contentment will become stronger, the moments of sorrow more shallow, less potent. Or maybe He'll simply ask me to obey and follow Him, period. No questions answered.

If He came to me tomorrow and said, "Sharyn, I have not ordained marriage for you so that I might be glorified through your singleness," I need to be obedient to that and thank Him for everything He has given me.

In the meantime, I hope. I hope I follow His plan for my life, and I don't try to take control. I hope God will give me the strength and grace I need to follow Him wholeheartedly, regardless of my circumstances. And I hope I always remember *He's* the goal—the reason I live.

Do you remember that quote I shared in chapter three from *Indiana Jones and the Last Crusade*: "It's time for you to decide what you believe"?

It's taken me a decade or two, but I've decided what I believe: God loves me. He has good things for me. Even in His silence, I can trust Him. I choose to believe this on a regular basis, and it seems to be working. Yes, some days making that choice feels like deciding to put a beloved dying dog to sleep, but I know it's right. On those days I still cry, feel the ache, then hand it to God and say, "I know what I believe."

In chapter eight I quoted the middle of John 16:33—"In this world you will have trouble." These words were spoken by Jesus, part of a warning that things were about to get worse for His apostles. But the warning is surrounded by hope. Here's the whole verse:

"I have told you these things, so that in Me you may have peace. In this world you will have trouble. But take heart! I have overcome the world."

We are overcomers because of Christ.

Through all of this, I hope you've found peace. I hope you've sensed God's hand on your life and have come to recognize how much He loves you. This is the truth.

Truth you can find your hope in.

Now, It's Your Turn

- What do you choose to believe about God and your singleness? Write it down. Then, if it's positive, remind yourself of these thoughts regularly, remembering it's a *choice*.

- Do you find it easy or difficult to put your hope in God where marriage is concerned? Expound on your answer.

- Can you accept your singleness if that's God's will for you? What makes this hard? What makes it easy?

- Have you spent specific, focused time with God, whether it included fasting or not? What did you learn during that time?

- What does the word "hope" mean to you? Look up Bible verses about hope—like 1 Cor. 15:19, 2 Cor. 4:16–18, Romans 8:24–25, and, indirectly, Zeph. 3:17.

- Has a husband been your goal and God the means to getting it? If so, what can you do today to make God the prize, not a man? Does this idea change your thinking about marriage? If so, how?

Postscript—

To Married Women
That's What Friends Are For

Friendship is certainly the finest balm
for the pangs of disappointed love.
        —Jane Austen, *Northanger Abbey*

It's hard—nearly impossible at times—to talk to our married friends about the struggles and heartaches of being still single and childless and abstinent and, often, alone. They think we're so lucky with our quiet, stress-free lives and wild weekend parties. They tell us things like, "You just need to work on your relationship with God and when that's good, He'll bring the perfect guy to your door!"

Right. Because marriage is the reward for getting our act together.

I've not only had people tell me as much, but it seems to be a popular platitude handed out to singles at church and family reunions and, most recently, in cute little memes plastered all over Facebook. While we're not supposed to be sad on the one hand, on the other, we must not be living a godly life or we'd be married already. Most of the time it hurts too much to try to explain, and I simply choose to avoid the topic in "mixed" company.

But what if we could communicate our ache? What if our married friends were more aware of the clichés and how they make us feel? What if we could let them know there are moments when it's hard for us to hear about date night with the husband or how cute their kids are? Not that we *can't* be a part of it, but some days our hearts are closer to breaking over our loss. When that happens we need sympathy and support, not pity or platitudes. We want to be a part of our married friends' lives and happiness, while still feeling our own heartaches and longings are understood.

So I'm going to talk to you now, woman-to-woman, and see if we can work this out.

Let's start with something I've only recently noticed: It seems to me that you talk differently about marriage with singles than you do with everyone else. I've heard married women warn us against even wanting to marry. The most common cliché is "it's better to be single than to be married to the wrong man." I'll get to that in a bit.

That's bad enough but it's just the beginning. We hear how hard it is to live with a man and how married couples fight and that a wedding ring won't make us happy. We're told being married is just like being single only with more dishes and laundry. We hear about lying husbands, affairs, domestic abuse, and divorce.

But then we see your posts online or hear you when you don't realize a single woman is listening and you talk about how much you love your husband, your best friend, your soul mate. You say you can't imagine your life without him. You see the love between a husband and wife as a beautiful, forever, God-ordained union.

You may think you're doing us a favor by emphasizing the potential downsides of matrimony, but we're not fooled. We realize marriage is tough and frustrating and sometimes he doesn't listen. We are aware of the fact that a husband will argue with us about money or insist on watching three different sporting events at once. But we also know it's sweet and secure and so wonderful the rest of the time. Okay, maybe not *all* of the rest of the time, but it must be nice to have someone to hash things out with, who will loan you his jacket when you're cold, who understands you better than anyone else. Who loves you enough to want to spend his life with you.

When you tell us being single is better than a bad marriage it honestly doesn't mean as much as you might imagine. Though I understand why people say it, I don't think it's a fair exchange. Can we *not* assume we'd pick the wrong guy? I'd like to think I'm as capable of recognizing a good man as any other mature woman with a decent head on her shoulders. Isn't it reasonable to think I could find someone as wonderful as all of those great husbands of so many of my friends? If I've gone this long without settling, it seems a safe bet I won't cave and get myself hitched to the next available loser to come along.

We all make mistakes, including marrying someone toxic. But isn't this the same as saying, "It's better to not have children than to have a bad one," or "An awful job is better than no job at all"? In each case, comments like this imply we shouldn't want things to be different on the off-chance different might be worse.

Even though, often, different is better.

But there is another side to this.

A few years ago, a single friend was chatting with a group of married women who were discussing an older, troubled, messed-up, single man at their church. They finally came to the conclusion that all he really needed was "a good woman."

Stunned, it took her a moment to respond. Then she asked, "Why would you wish *that* on a good woman?!"

This is another of those married-people conundrums: They warn us against the nightmare of marrying the wrong man in one breath and, in the next, try to match us up with the poor, unmotivated, lonely schmuck who still lives with his mom and smells like bologna. I don't mean to be harsh—everyone deserves love. Just don't set us up with someone who doesn't want the same things we do.

Most of us dream of a partner, not a project. Yes, some single women *are* desperate enough to settle for the wrong guy. Be on the lookout for that tendency in unmarried friends and, if necessary and possible, talk her down from the ledge. As you know, though, women sometimes put on rose-colored glasses when it comes to men, which makes those red flags so much harder to see. Sometimes all you can do is pray.

Now, back to this whole idea that we need to be warned away from our dreams of floating down the aisle in a whirly-twirly ivory dress with a handkerchief hem. (Well, that's what I always wanted anyway.) Please don't assume our singleness means we are naïve to the realities of marriage. We don't gaze out windows with pie-in-the-sky ideals, sighing as we dream of white knights and winsome words and wedded bliss. We know it will be hard. Like being single is hard. Like being human is hard.

But we're not afraid of it.

I, personally, would welcome the challenge to be less self-centered. To be forced, on a daily basis, to put someone else's needs above my own. I've done the all-by-myself, eat-when-I-want, do-what-I-want, live-how-I-want long enough. Whenever I hear single people say doing whatever you want is one of the best reasons to be single, I cringe. Selfishness is not a blessing. It's not something to cheer and be proud of. I'm ready to be a part of something more intimate in my relationships, more giving, more him and *Him* and less me.

And you know what? It's okay for a single person to want to tie the knot. Say what you will, but marriage is a good thing, ordained and blessed by God. Wanting it is perfectly natural. God made me this way. He gave me a romantic heart and a longing for a man. Yes, it's part of the Genesis curse: "Your desire shall be for your husband" (Gen. 3:16b), but it's also a blessing: "Marriage is honorable among all, and the bed undefiled ..." (Heb. 13:4a) and "He who finds a wife finds a good thing, and obtains favor from the LORD" (Prov. 18:22).

Do I want to be a good man's "good thing"? Oh, yes, I do. And there's nothing wrong with that.

Please don't try to "fix" us. We're not broken. Perhaps a little scratched and bruised, maybe somewhat tattered, but who isn't?

Our spiritual needs are the same as yours. Saying something like, "You need to work on your relationship with God. Get that right, and then He'll bring you a man," doesn't help. First, who *doesn't* need to work on their relationship with God? And second, does anyone ever get it right? Shouldn't we spend our life pursuing a closer, more intimate relationship with Him? You certainly shouldn't put all that aside the moment a minister says, "I now pronounce you husband and wife."

Last—but far from least—*you don't know God will bring someone a spouse.* That might not be His plan. Like I said: a husband is not a reward for finally figuring things out.

We should avoid the inference that married women have their spiritual life under control and they're ready for heaven. As if having a husband proves their faith. This is dangerous because it not only could give married women freedom to forget about God, but it puts the burden of "It's all your fault" on singles. Again, marriage is no more a prize because someone has managed a perfect, holy life than singleness is punishment for not being a strong enough Christian.

Being single is not a sign we've messed up or failed in our faith. There isn't a "formula" for this. God hasn't set up some cosmic brain-tease marriage test that we have to pass before He grants our wish and blesses us with a man.

Speaking of tests, I want to say something about this to my single friends. ...

The Great Marriage Eligibility Test

You know how they say a man will come along as soon as you stop looking and you think, "Well, I guess no man will ever come along because I'll never stop looking," but then, one day, you discuss with some friends how you don't know what the next year will bring and one says, "Yeah, you might be married by then" and, for the first time in your life, you think that might not be what you want anymore and you freak out, just a little, since you're no longer sure you want to get married because of the direction God's leading your ministry, and piggy-backing on that thought is this:

"Wait ... if I'm no longer certain I want to get married does that mean I'm finally *not* looking so now God will bring me a man?"

Then you think, "I guess I *am* still looking after all."

And you sigh and shrug and figure you failed the test once again. After all, God will bring you a man when you stop looking. That's what everyone says, right?

Everyone else wants to find a reason for why we're single just like we do. As previously mentioned, there's the oldie but goodie: "You probably need to work on your relationship with God." Or you need to lose weight or get out of debt or _____ (fill in the blank).

Bottom line: You're a mess. And who wants to marry a mess?

All of which sets up this underlying idea that we're single because we haven't figured out The Secret yet. We still haven't passed The Great Marriage Eligibility Test. Every five minutes or so you meet some cute, young thing who's married but definitely does *not* have her act together, and you think, "*She* passed the test?! How did she pass, but I didn't?"

Well, I'm going to say something you might not like, but hang in there with me: It *is* a test, though not one to see if you're ready for marriage or not. It's a test to see if you will trust God, whatever happens.

Here's the good news: This kind of testing is part of the whole faith experience. Paul even encouraged us in how to handle it:

> *So we do not lose heart. Though our outer self is wasting away, our inner self is being renewed day by day. For this light momentary affliction is preparing for us an eternal weight of glory beyond all comparison, as we look not to the things that are seen but to the things that are unseen. For the things that are seen are transient, but the things that are unseen are eternal* (2 Cor. 4:16–18, ESV).

Not everyone is strong enough to handle such a test, but God knew you could. I'm not saying this is the only reason you're single. I am saying, though, that the next time someone tells you you're single because you haven't stopped looking or your relationship with God needs work or they throw some new and improved test question at you, just smile serenely and tell them:

"That's not the test I'm working on."

Yes, God has a reason for our singleness and it's quite possible we will never know what that reason is. Having someone tell us it's because we've failed in our relationship with Him only adds salt to the wound.

Home for the Holidays

A friend of mine once mentioned on Facebook how much she dreads Christmas. To her it's a red beacon of family-togetherness, flashing the reminder that she doesn't have one. Well-meaning friends encouraged her to spend time with loved ones or volunteer to serve others.

This is good advice. In fact, these are about the best suggestions you can give. But it's Band-Aid advice. It covers and protects and can even provide a measure of healing. Yet the wound—at the end of the day—will still be there.

Some singles spend major holidays by themselves, some with family or friends, some volunteer, but most of us grieve something on those days. No matter what we give or how much joy we share, we will, eventually, go home alone. We'll put our holiday dishes away in silence. We'll spoon any leftovers we grabbed into individual containers and cram them in the freezer. We'll crawl between cold sheets and hug an extra pillow to our chests for warmth.

You can't fix that or change it. This is our wound. And sometimes, especially over the holidays, it rips open, exposing us to the rawness of our loneliness.

For me, Christmas and Mother's Day are the roughest. Christmas because it has such a romantic quality and I want to share it with someone on a more intimate level. That's why The Hallmark Channel does so well with romantic movies at that time of year.

Mother's Day is far worse, though, because my mom is gone and I don't have children of my own. I learned the hard way not to go to church on that day. When the pastor has all the different types of mothers stand, single women can find themselves the only ones still sitting, surrounded by men and sorrow. It would hurt less to just run us down with a Zamboni.

A Tuna Casserole Would Have Been Nice

Years ago, while working at a large company, I started feeling ill right after the New Year began. Thinking it was an ulcer, I went to the doctor. He told me it was actually my gall bladder and scheduled to remove it the next day, which was a Wednesday. If all had gone well, I would have been back to work the following Monday.

All did not go well, though, and on Monday, pain in my left calf took me back to the doctor's office. Thanks to an ultrasound, they discovered I had developed blood clots. This meant two weeks of bed rest. I had to keep my legs elevated, give myself shots in my stomach every day, and have my blood drawn by a visiting nurse, also every day.

In my time with this company, I had seen many people end up away from the office for days, even weeks, because of illness. Every time, a sign-up sheet would go around to take them meals. Most of my co-workers had spouses to help out, but we still gladly did what we could to make things easier. Seeing as I wasn't supposed to stand longer than necessary, I anticipated something similar when I told them my situation.

They didn't even check up on me. No one asked me how I was doing. I had to make do on cans of soup and peanut butter and jelly sandwiches. I was fine of course; I didn't go hungry. But it hurt. It still hurts. I was lonely and bored, in pain, and a little scared. Yet my singleness gave them the impression I didn't need help. I didn't have a hungry husband and kids, so why would they need to make me a tuna casserole or even bring me a pizza? Or maybe they just forgot.

Neither answer makes me feel any better.

By the way, one friend did come over with her daughters and cleaned my house for me, which I greatly appreciated. Still ... it was a long two weeks. Being sick and bed/couch-ridden is as difficult for singles as it is for married folk. Maybe it's a different kind of difficult but, in many ways, it's the same.

True or False

Every time I hear a married person speak about being single it reminds me married people shouldn't speak about being single. There may be a few exceptions, but, for the most part, they don't get it. Whether they have the best intentions—e.g. to help you focus on your relationship with God; or they have misguided ones—e.g. to talk you out of wanting to get married—their perspective is off. They talk about singleness as they see singleness: through the eyes of a married man or woman.

Think I'm wrong? When was the last time you heard a single person talking to married couples about marriage?

Most of the time, these "I'm-married-you're-not" sermons come across as condescending. They have a list of things they think we've fallen for and they're here to set us straight. God bless 'em.

I want to take a moment to clear up two myths some people might believe when it comes to being single.

Let's start with the concern that we're making marriage an idol. This is a harsh accusation, considering the first of the Ten Commandments: "You shall have no other gods before Me" (Exodus 20:3). But is wanting to marry making an idol of it?

In her book *Get Married: What Women Can Do to Help It Happen*, author Candice Watters wrote: "Scripture is clear: idolatry has everything to do with our earthly nature, evil desires, wrong motives, and pursuit of our own pleasures."

Does marriage as God intended fit into that description?

She goes on to say, "Not only is it unlikely that a godly woman's desire for a biblical marriage would become an idol, biblical marriage is the antidote to much of the idolatry—'sexual immorality, impurity, lust, evil desires and greed'—that plagues our culture."

Is it wrong to want a better job or a nicer home or happy, healthy children? No. God knows we will pursue those things. The problem comes when we put our pursuit of anything ahead of our pursuit of Him.

Please don't assume that's what we're doing with our marriage dreams.

Another myth is the idea that we think matrimony will solve all our problems. But the thing is, it *will* solve some of them. How could it not? The whole sex issue comes to mind. Sharing a home and expenses on two incomes instead of one would certainly help financially. We can work on the house together, share driving duties on long trips, and hold each other's hands during the difficult days.

All of which takes me back to what I alluded to earlier: Please don't think our singleness means we don't know how to handle a complex, adult relationship. We have the ability to figure it out, much like you did. And when we hit hard times with our husbands—and we will—we'll learn and grow and, hopefully, become better people because of it.

But we need your heart to be tender toward our hearts to get through the tough times.

A few years ago, a friend lost her mother to a brain tumor. At the funeral, in the midst of her grief, a woman approached her and said, "It's just so sad you never married. I know that's something she always wanted for you."

This is the kind of thing no one needs to tell us. We don't need to hear we're getting past our prime or a good man is hard to find or we're breaking our mother's heart by remaining single.

We know you love us and we choose to believe you want to encourage and support us in our singleness. That's why I'm pointing these things out.

To recap:

- **Don't** tiptoe around us like we're fragile children. Treat us like adults who can figure things out and work through them. Singleness does *not* equal immaturity.

- **Don't** claim you know there's someone out there for us. That leads to false hope. The only one who *knows* if that's true is God.

- Please **don't** repeat clichés about singleness. We've heard them all and have already decided how we feel about each one.

- **Do** let us be sad and offer a shoulder to cry on.

- **Do** tell us about great single men you know. We realize it's one of the best ways to meet new guys. Most of us are open to a set-up with a good man, just tell us ahead of time. Surprise blind dates are, more often than not, awkward for everyone. Just make sure—I implore you—that he *is* a good man.

- **Do** encourage us to hope but not to obsess; help us through heartbreak and over bad days.

- **Do** check up on us when we're sick. Offering to pick up medicine or even a carton of orange juice would mean so much!

- **Do** pray for us.

But why not do something a little more? Take this advice, for instance, from writer Christena Cleveland (christenacleveland.com, "Singled Out: How Churches Can Embrace Unmarried Adults"):

If you get married and/or have a baby, Christians will pull out all the stops to celebrate you. That's a good thing! But Christians should also recognize that many single adults never get celebrated with such fanfare. We might not be walking down the aisle or gestating a baby, but God is doing some amazing things in our lives—from the "monumental" (such as helping us obtain degrees, launch ministries/businesses, pay off college loans) to the "mundane" (such as helping us serve our neighborhoods, pray for each other).

We must celebrate what God's doing in people's lives, whether it's similar to what God's done in our own lives or not. So, find reasons to throw big parties for the single people in your community. And if you have the resources, feel free to buy them expensive gifts as well.

Single people use Kitchen Aid mixers too.

We still need you.

I need you. My singleness is not a sign of selfish independence. I know you might have trouble understanding what it's like, which is why I'm not asking for empathy. I'm asking for your camaraderie and support as my sister-friend in Christ.

We're all in this together. The fact that you're still reading shows how much you love and care for your single friends.

Thank you for sticking by us through the ups and downs of spinsterhood. Personally, I don't know what I'd do without the married women in my life. You give me hope.

Because if you can do it and survive, maybe I can too.

Now, It's Your Turn

- What do you think of the clichés I mentioned? Have you said/heard any of them before? Did they come from married or single friends?

- Which suggestion surprised you the most? Why?

- Does this give you a better understanding of what single women go through? If so, how?

- If you're single, are there any myths you would add that you feel married women believe? What are they and how do you feel about them?

- What are some things married and single women can do to support and encourage each other? Brainstorm for a bit ... and then, if possible, do them!

Endnotes

Anderson, Lisa. "Finding a Great Husband Doesn't Just 'Happen'." *Today's Christian Woman*, November 26, 2013.

Cleveland, Christena. "Singled Out: How Churches Can Embrace Unmarried Adults." *christenacleveland.com*, 2013.

Eldredge, John. *Wild at Heart: Discovering the Secret of a Man's Soul*. Nashville, TN: Thomas Nelson, 2001.

Lewis, C.S. *The Four Loves*. New York: Harcourt, Brace, 1960.

Tierney, John. "2004: In a Word; Adultescent." *New York Times*, December 26, 2004.

Watters, Candice. *Get Married: What Women Can Do to Help It Happen*. Chicago: Moody Publishers, 2008.

Made in the USA
Columbia, SC
24 January 2019